Untangled

You're not stuck. You're not lost. You're not a hot mess.

You just need to
GET UNTANGLED.

MYCHELLE FERNANDEZ

What People are Saying about Untangled

"Mychelle Fernandez provides a refreshing look at creating your next best life in *Untangled*. If you have ever felt overwhelmed, underappreciated, guilty, or just plain lost, this book will guide you to finding the light, love, and confidence within yourself and then how to reveal it to the world around you."

Sharon Lechter, Author of *Think and Grow Rich for Women,* Co-Author of *Rich Dad Poor Dad,* 14 other books in the Rich Dad Series, *Exit Rich, Three Feet from Gold, Outwitting the Devil, Success and Something Greater*

"Mychelle and the Working Moms Tribe Movement can help your organization craft solutions that will help attract and retain highly talented working mom assets."-*

Patty Aubery, President, The Jack Canfield Companies #1 New York Times Best-Selling Author

"This book is the secret weapon that every working mom can use to help them strive to achieve clarity and purpose in their lives. Mychelle Fernandez has put together a unique collection of inspirational tips and life strategies, in an easy-to-read guide. Her book is incredibly noteworthy and so valuable to working moms in today's busy world! *Untangled* is truly magical! Well done!"

John Formica, The "Ex-Disney Guy", America's Customer Experience Speaker, Trainer & Coach

"Mychelle is such an inspiration to dream big and make the shifts necessary to make progress!"

Joe Theismann, World Champion and Entrepreneur

"I love the approach Mychelle recommends to help me find my confidence, courage, and clarity!"

Jill Lublin, International Speaker, 4x Best-Selling Author, & Master Publicity Strategist

All glory and honor to God, who gives me strength. Thank you for your unending grace and mercy, for choosing and loving me, and never leaving my side or letting go of my hand. Bless and heal every mom that comes across this book so she may be moved to bless and heal others.

To my husband and biggest supporter, Dover. Thank you for always believing in me and encouraging me to follow my heart and chase my big dreams. I love the life God has guided us to create together.

To my children Chase, Andi, Ryan, & Ensley. Thank you for filling my world with so much color, light, and love and for being my unending source of inspiration. I'm so blessed to be your mom.

To my mom Rose who showed me how to overcome and get untangled by faithfully trusting God. Thank you for giving me the life and experiences you gave.

MOTIVATE AND INSPIRE OTHERS!

"Share This Book"

Retail $24.95

Special Quantity Discounts

5-20 Books	$21.95
21-99 Books	$18.95
100-499 Books	$15.95
500-999 Books	$10.95
1,000+ Books	$8.95

To Place an Order Contact:
info@workingmomstribe.org

(858) 221-6900 or (866) 995 -5858

The Ideal Professional Speaker For Your Next Event!

Any organization that wants to positively shift the V.I.B.E. (vision, identity, balance, and energy) of their people needs to hire Mychelle for a keynote and/or workshop training!

To Contact or Book Mychelle to Speak:

info@workingmomstribe.org

Call or text; (858) 221-6900

Call or fax: (866) 995-5858

www.workingmomstribe.org

Contents

Introduction

BECAUSE I WAS made for more. That is the response I wish I could have given every time someone asked me why I left one position for another. In the two decades following college, I held 10 professional level positions. On average, I lasted about two years at a position before I found a reason to move on to a new one. Most of the time it was shorter than that. Many people warned me that if I didn't stay longer at each position, potential employers might view me as a flight risk and not hire me. Yet somehow, recruiters and hiring managers still invited me to apply and interview and I continued to be offered positions with some of the most well-known companies in the world. Each time I started a new position with one of these amazing companies, I was humbled and grateful. It felt exciting to be part of the amazing innovation and magic that was happening at these organizations. I wanted to love it, develop strong roots, and grow with these companies. I worked with talented, down-to-earth people, the companies offered great opportunities and benefits, and my skillset and experience were a good fit. However, each time, something didn't feel quite right. It was an odd feeling. Where I had been, the companies, the projects, the levels, the titles, and the salaries, all made me feel very accomplished, yet I felt so unfulfilled. Whenever that feeling would creep in, I would think to myself, "Ugh, not again. What's wrong with me? Why do I keep coming to this point?" I felt like I was just repeating a cycle and not learning or growing. Ironically, that is exactly what I told hiring managers I was seeking each time I interviewed for a new role; an opportunity that would allow me to learn and grow. Instead, I felt like a hamster running in a hamster wheel, burning energy, getting tired, but not getting anywhere. I felt so lost and confused. More than anything, I felt stuck. I knew I wasn't actually stuck, but I felt that way. I stopped working a few times, thinking maybe I was just burnt out and needed a break. I'd return to work a few months later only to find myself feeling the same way I felt the day I left.

It took several years to sort out why I kept coming to this point. The main issue was that I wasn't stepping into my purpose, and that's because I didn't even know what it was. I never even stopped to reflect on my purpose. I mistook my goals and aspirations for my God-given purpose. I may have reached and exceeded my goals, but my intuition knew God had something different, something more planned for me. The signs were all there, but without knowing what the future held for me, I was too scared to explore anything too far beyond what I knew and was comfortable with. I learned the hard way that you can try to control your life all you want, but what is meant to be will be. After the right combination and sequence of events, I eventually surrendered and sat still and quiet enough to hear whispers of other possibilities. The Working Moms Tribe Movement was the idea that came through the loudest. It was needed, and it was exciting, but I wasn't confident I was right for this job. After waiting and receiving enough signs, I trusted and moved forward with both fear and confidence. I had to keep reminding myself God had never failed me before and to believe he would continue to equip and guide me. Slowly and surely, He did, and here we are today, gaining momentum and building the Movement that provides personal and professional development support and resources to working moms and teaches employers how to work collaboratively with their working mom assets.

During the time I had paused to be still, it gave me time to get to things that were low on my priority list, like organizing my necklace collection. I love necklaces and own dozens of them. They are mostly casual, fashion jewelry pieces, but there are some fine jewelry pieces in my collection too. I've collected them over so many years but never took the time to come up with a good system to store and organize them. As my collection grew, I would attempt to use organizers and storage containers to keep them all together. I had a hanging jewelry cabinet, a pegboard with random hooks, and several tabletop jewelry organizers to hang them. There was no rhyme or reason to what went where, as long as they ended up in my closet. The problem was I couldn't remember all the necklaces I had or where I put them. When I get ready, my accessories are the last things I put on before I leave the house. Often trying to find the right necklace and getting it untangled from other necklaces would make me late. I remember buying the perfect red necklace for an outfit I was going to wear on a gameshow, only to discover I already owned a similar piece better than the new one I bought! This is what prompted me to find a better system to store and organize my necklace collection. Being mindful of time and budget constraints, I used white grid wall panels and hooks to solve the problem. After sorting through and organizing them, the left half of my closet looked like a wall of a fashion jewelry store. Standing back to look up at this vast wall of necklaces organized and displayed by color, style, and size, I saw a parallel between them and my journey.

Each necklace is like a story, an experience, an identity, or an energy. Each brought me so much joy or were with me during a trying time in my life. Yet, in the hustle and bustle of life, I would carelessly put them away after each use, allowing them to break, get lost, or tangled. The organizing project allowed me to go through, sort, repair, and untangle them. Instead of tarnished, randomly grouped clumps of chains, beads, stones, and gems, I can now see and find the perfect piece to complete each of my outfits. Finding and stepping into my purpose was a similar process. I had to reflect on my story, my experiences, and my different identities. It helped me realize I was not stuck or lost; I was just tangled! I just needed the right purpose and system to get untangled. Looking back at my journey, I understand and appreciate each experience and the different identities I've assumed along the way. They are each valuable and play an important role in allowing me to find and live my unique purpose.

You may experience similar moments of feeling lost, stuck, overwhelmed, or unfocused. Wherever you are in this moment is a necessary stop in your unique journey. The life of a working mom doesn't leave much room or time to properly sort out and appreciate our "necklace" collection of experiences. As a result, we might get tangled not seeing the connections between where we've been and where we are going. With purpose and the right habits, you can get untangled and moving forward again. As you read through the chapters and reflect on your journey, may you embrace how strong, resilient, appreciative, humble, and cautious you have become because of it. You learned, and you grew. Along the way, you've built up your unique and perfect "necklace" collection to weather each storm and celebrate each victory. This book will facilitate the part of your journey where you get untangled and find your confidence, courage, and clarity again. It will also help you develop useful habits to keep them within reach when life makes it hard to see and appreciate the value of your journey.

Reflection

Take 10 minutes to create a timeline highlighting the major events in your life that have shaped who you have become (or are becoming).

"If you're in a place, physically or in your own head, that makes you strive for perfection, try to shift to a place that fosters *progress* instead."

WORKING MOMS
TRIBE

CHAPTER ONE

Start Small

WHEN STARTING SOMETHING new, it's easier to talk yourself out of starting than it is to actually start. New things are foreign, awkward, and uncomfortable. Everything you're good at now was once new, foreign, and maybe even hard when you first started. With time and practice, it got easier. So even if you don't know where to start, just start, and remember it will become familiar and get easier. To make it less intimidating and to help set yourself up for success, start small. Start small. It's a reminder I will repeat several times throughout this book. Sometimes you just need a little momentum to get started. Other times, you might need to break things down to the smallest, easiest steps to get started. Breaking things down into smaller, doable steps helps to overcome mental and physical hurdles. Never discredit these small, seemingly mundane steps. Not only do those small steps keep things moving, but they are also necessary. They are what transform effort into outcome. The small steps are how the hard things get done. As I like to think of it, small steps add up to big wins. Small steps make up the systems and habits that lead to progress and success.

We are all on different journeys and different phases of our journeys. That first small step might be mental, or it might be physical. It might be believing you will get to the finish line or it might be getting out of bed in the morning. Whatever that first or next step is, take it. If you can't, ask yourself why. Can and does the step need to be broken down into smaller steps? The objective is forward progress. When several necklaces become tangled, freeing one necklace probably won't free them all at once. You have to work on sections or knots one at time. Slowly the knots will become undone and the ball will loosen, making it easier to untangle. You might work on a certain knot or area with little to no progress. Sometimes you might need to take a fresh approach or work on another area to make progress. Getting untangled requires trial, error, and lots of patience. It might be slower than you hope for, but it will be worthwhile.

Reading this book might be the step you needed in the right direction. You can easily read one chapter a day and get a few ideas on what your next step(s) could be. I want to caution you on how circumstances might try to impede your progress before you feel or see the progress you've made. Circumstances will come along to plant seeds of discouragement and doubt. They will make you feel like the steps you've taken aren't big enough or don't matter. They will make you question if you have what it takes to get to the finish line. Try to think of circumstances as microscopes or magnifying glasses that help you see the areas of your life that needed support or improvement. They do it by wearing you down and stripping things away until you're forced to be strong, courageous, resilient, or whatever you're supposed to be. Circumstances increase your awareness of the skills, identities, and experiences you already have within you. Look past these minor setbacks and keep taking the small steps that build and grow your abilities and keep you moving forward.

When you're untangled, circumstances will lose their grip on you. You won't need them to remind you of what you have within you. You'll be clearer on who you are, where you've been, and the tools you've picked up along the way. You'll be able to remind yourself that you are a fierce working mom forged by the many experiences that shaped you, especially the ones that made you a mom. If you think about all the small steps that led to you becoming a mom, you will be reminded how incredibly amazing and capable you are. Whether by accident, months of planning, natural conception, fertility treatment or support, adoption, or other choices or circumstances, becoming a mom was a complex process that involved a series of decisions and small steps. It was foreign. You were filled with fear, worry, uncertainty, and doubt. Yet here you are. Somehow you took each step and figured it out as you went.

So before giving up, either before you even started or because you're discouraged, remind yourself. I've faced and conquered new and scary before. I have been uncomfortable with new and scary things before. I learned, I grew, and became comfortable. I figured it out and overcame, and I can do it again. Keep taking the small steps. The confidence, courage, and clarity will naturally follow, and your small steps will get bigger, and soon enough you'll be making leaps and bounds.

Reflection

Think of a time in your life that felt uncomfortable or uneasy because it required you to learn or experience something new (or a perceived failure) that ultimately led to a positive experience or mastery of a new skill. Write about it reflecting on the steps you had to take and when and how it become comfortable, familiar, or easy?

CHAPTER TWO

The Framework

WHEN I FINALLY got around to organizing my necklaces, I loosely followed the 5S approach. The 5S approach is derived from a Japanese methodology to organize the workplace to maximize efficiency. Translated into English, the 5 S's stand for sort, set in order, shine, standardize, and sustain. I started by physically untangling and separating the necklaces. I pulled out broken necklaces and those that no longer brought me joy. I donated the ones I no longer wanted and repaired the broken ones. Then I hung them on the grid wall, arranging them in a way that was both aesthetically pleasing and easiest to access them and put them away. If they were necklaces I used less frequently, the really loud, chunky ones, I displayed and stored them up high. I moved things around and adjusted until each piece had a place, one that I could easily locate and access when I needed it. Despite all my personality, behavior, and strengths assessments indicating that I do not do well with formality and structure and my need for flexibility, I know and understand the value of systems and organization. Systems and organization help to streamline processes, saving time, money, and energy, and improving efficiency, and productivity, which all help the bottom line. Systems help manage the resources needed and coming in and the output. In a working mom's life, it helps you see what is left at the end of the day. It's the net loss or gain after being emptied by others and refueling yourself. It's worth taking a moment to reflect on what that currently looks like. Do most of your days close with a net positive or negative gain? Or do you feel like most days you're breaking even?

I was thinking about the best way to help you systematize this process of getting (and staying) untangled. We are all at different points in our journey to find and live our purpose. I've loosely structured this book to help you:

1. unpack and untangle the experiences you've had and the ideas, gifts, skills, and identities you've discovered along your journey;

2. take an inventory of them, deciding which ones to focus on and refine and which ones to let go of;

3. keep them visible and accessible; and

4. use, connect, leverage, and share them when needed.

I will guide and help you create a system that makes the most sense for you. Ultimately, you will design your system to fit your needs. I will give you ideas and remind you to keep it simple and doable. The last thing you need is another competing interest demanding more of your time and energy. The approach I teach comprises one small step after another. I help you assess four general areas of your life so you can determine where to focus your attention. I share practices that have worked for me to help you identify new behaviors to try. As you recognize which ones give you results, you can slowly incorporate them into your system, repeating the ones that help you feel untangled until they become habits. I've also created different journals you can use to reflect, capture thoughts and new ideas, and monitor progress. Be mindful of even brief moments of feeling untangled and what helped you to feel that way. Try to amplify or expand those moments by being intentional to do more of whatever helped you feel that way. Untangled to you might feel like clarity, calm, peace, joy, or a combination of these things. Note any actions, practices, or behaviors associated with those untangled feelings. They should be intentionally incorporated or designed into your system. Your system might be a daily morning routine or a weekly routine with essential elements that can be more loosely scheduled in. As you identify the right habits, find the times and places to make them easy to incorporate.

Reflection

Are there small steps that you can start to develop into habits and your system for getting untangled? Is there anything you know you need to let go of to help you get untangled?

"We have the power to *stop the hurt* from spreading."

WORKING MOMS
TRIBE

CHAPTER THREE

Create Your Own Current

AS YOU GET untangled and develop your system to stay untangled, moving onward and up, remember to keep the focus on you. Your career, your family, your friends, and anything or anyone else that you give your time to, can dictate your schedule and where you are going if you allow them to. As you read this book, intentionally give yourself time to reflect on you and what helps you to feel the most untangled and free. It is how you feel when you are being the best version of yourself. When you are not intentional about giving energy to your purpose and where it requires you to go, it's easy to get caught in the fast-moving currents of those around you.

Many working moms, or women in general, often feel like they are not enough. We live in a world full of propaganda aimed at selling us products and services businesses want us to believe we need. Social media has provided a platform to distribute facades faster and wider. It makes it challenging to find our voice and purpose and be happy and grateful for where we are at the moment. The next time you feel bad about yourself, become overwhelmed with mom-guilt, or don't feel you're enough, take a moment to think about what or who you are judging yourself against. Chances are, they don't have the same children, significant other, job, gifts, experiences, values, beliefs, friends, or dreams as you. Comparing yourself to anything or anyone other than who you were yesterday is not an accurate measure of progress and will likely set yourself up for disappointment. If comparison to others is a habit you've picked up along the way, now is the time to drop it!

When I started college, I didn't know what I wanted to pursue, so I followed the recommendations of my family and teachers. I started at UCLA as a pre-med student and majored in chemistry. When people asked, I told them I wanted to be an anesthesiologist. About a year into the program, I realized the behaviors and competition around me did not resonate with me. I could not see myself in that world. I changed my major to biochemistry (mostly to avoid multivariable calculus) and explored what else I could do that was respectable and lucrative. My last year in college, I came across a student worker position in a crime lab in Los Angeles. During the hiring process, I decided it was the career I wanted to pursue after college, a criminalist, more commonly referred to as a crime scene investigator or "CSI". The first CSI TV show had just aired a few months before and that show made it seem like a very glamorous career. They hired me and assigned me to the serological unit. DNA analysis was in its infancy but was making tremendous advances and quickly. During my time with the crime lab, they resurrected backlogs of cold cases to see if DNA analysis could shed new light on the stale, unsolved cases. My job was to calibrate laboratory equipment, prepare buffers and reagents for the criminalists, and process evidence analysis requests from the detectives. It was exciting to see how science was being used to help solve crimes and to be a part of it. When I graduated from UCLA, I applied for one of the criminalist positions with the same crime lab. I had to take a written exam as part of the application process, and I scored fairly high for my first time. I had a significant chance of getting hired considering the hiring managers knew me, I had a very relevant degree, and the number of positions available. Had I stayed the course, I might have been a supervising criminalist today. Two things changed my course. The police department had a hiring freeze and froze the criminalist positions. I also met my (now) husband and started dating him. He lived in my hometown, San Diego, two-and-a-half hours south of Los Angeles. I moved back to San Diego, started a master's program in chemistry, and got a job at a biotech company doing research and development involving new nucleic acid technology. I figured the master's degree and relevant work experience with DNA would make me more qualified when criminalist positions opened up again.

I got married while working on my master's degree and working on the lab bench. My husband graduated the year we got married and was offered an engineering position that was rarely offered to new college grads. We could not pass up the opportunity. Without having the same foot in the door in any of the San Diego area crime labs and being unable to move back to Los Angeles because of my husband's job, the prospect of becoming a criminalist started to look grim. That marked the beginning of floundering from job to job, trying to figure out what else I could do and where I was supposed to be.

I went from product development experiments on a lab bench, to health inspecting for local government, to environmental, health, and safety (EHS) management for biotech, to worker and food safety at a major theme park, to EHS consulting. I deceived myself because I was moving forward and up. I eventually aimed for a director level EHS position. I got there, but when I did, it did not feel like that was where I was meant to be. It wasn't until I jumped out of the water, and out of the current of busyness that was hastily pushing me along, that I spent some time with myself to reflect on where I was going. Had I been as intentional back then about spending time with God and myself every morning as I am now, I'm sure I would have found my current, the one moving at my pace and in the direction meant for me, much sooner.

Reflection

Do you spend time with yourself on a regular basis to realign your days and activities with where you're aspiring to go? Is there anything you could do differently to improve the quality of that time?

"If all you have the *energy* for today is only enough to complete tiny things, it is *enough*."

WORKING MOMS
—— TRIBE ——

"*Small steps* make up the systems and habits that lead to *progress and success.*"

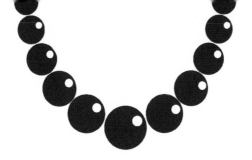

CHAPTER FOUR

Values

IN THIS BOOK, I share a lot of things I do or have done to help me get untangled. Some of them may not resonate with you and you may not be inclined to try. Identifying your personal values and core values cannot be one of them! At the root of many of the knots in your life is not knowing or honoring your values. Your personal values are the top 10-20 ideals you live by. They are the virtues you stand for. They communicate to others what is important to you. Your core values are the top five values that define your character and how you conduct yourself. I always thought I knew what my values were until I was asked to list them out loud. It was an exercise at one of my jobs, and it surprised me how long it took me to identify them from the list that they provided to us during the exercise. I am grateful that employer took the time to help us as employees get clear on our values. Little did I know that exercise would be part of my untangling process years later.

Company core values are something I often looked into while interviewing for new roles. They are one of the most widely available pieces of information companies include on their website. It was something to mention during the interview to show I had done my research on the companies. It wasn't until I did that exercise that I looked back and figured out how inconsistent some of my former employers were with their stated core values. From that point, I made it a point to ask questions about the company core values during the interview to see if employees knew what they were and if they aligned with company practices. I also became more cognizant of whether core values of companies that I might work for or do business with aligned with my core values or not. The misalignment of company core values with my core values and/or the company's inconsistency with their own core values helped to explain that gut feeling that told me when a company wasn't the right fit for me or when it was time to move on.

Aside from helping you figure out who to work for or do business with, core values help with other major decisions in life. Every major life decision should pass through your core values to avoid the potential of being put in positions that conflict with your core values down the line. Even if something doesn't perfectly align with your core values, being aware of it early gives you the opportunity to better prepare for conflicts that may arise in the future. When you are clear on your values, you invite the right people and opportunities into your life. Conversely, if you don't know what your values are, your decisions and actions will be inconsistent, and what you attract into your life might also be inconsistent and confusing. Values are the foundation of who you are, what you stand for, and what you stand against. They are the principles that tell you how to live your life to achieve what matters to you.

If you don't write out your values or you have never reflected on what they are, grab a pen and paper (right now) and start jotting down the principles that are most important to you. Once you identify your core values write them down somewhere you will see them often. I posted a list of values you can use as a starting point at www.workingmomstribe.org/values. It can also be helpful to ask your closest family and friends what they believe your core values are. This can help you understand how your actions have been perceived and if they align with the values you'd like to define and guide you. Clarity with things like your purpose, mission, and vision start with clarity of your personal and core values.

The Working Moms Tribe Movement core values are:

1. We SUPPORT each other's dreams, decisions, and journeys.

2. We foster authentic CONNECTION and relationships.

3. We cultivate LEADERSHIP skills.

4. We LOVE because we are loved.

5. We give ourselves and each other GRACE.

The Working Moms Tribe Movement mission is to connect and educate working moms and employers so they can better understand each other's perspectives and priorities and find creative ways to work together to acknowledge and support them.

The Working Moms Tribe Movement vision is to inspire perception shifts that will create and steward positive, purposeful, and joyful experiences for women who choose to have both a profession and a family.

My personal values are FAITH in God, FAMILY, INTEGRITY, SERVICE and GROWTH. They are much better aligned with what I am doing now than any of the positions I previously held. Honoring them has definitely helped me to avoid knots that might otherwise be difficult to untangle. I feel lightest, freest, and most at peace staying true to my core values.

Reflection

What are your top 10 personal values and your 5 core values? Place them where you will see them on a regular basis and commit them to memory so you can easily list them if ever asked.

CHAPTER FIVE

Find the Opportunity

I AM A believer of everything happening for a reason. When I look back at my journey, every experience fits perfectly into place, only able to interlock with the events immediately preceding and following it. As painful and difficult as some experiences may have been, there was purpose even in the pain and suffering. I have always landed in a better place than where I was, so I have no reason to believe my future will be any different. This comes with having an optimistic outlook. It has served me well, so I will continue to adopt it until it doesn't! This attitude is a direct reflection of my core values.

I have had too many uncanny "coincidences" happen in my life that I stopped believing in coincidences. Instead, I believe that there is a greater power at work connecting all the pieces at just the right time. For me, that greater power is God. I respect if you believe in coincidences, or the universe, or some other divine force. For me, it's God. Knowing that he is at work even when I can't see it has brought me peace during times that might otherwise trigger worry, panic, or anxiety.

Nelson Mandela once said, "I never lose. I either win or learn." I agree with him and this aligns with my core value of growth. As I mentioned earlier, I have always been able to find purpose in pain and suffering I've endured. I've learned that there is always an opportunity hidden beneath or behind adversity. It could be an opportunity to learn, grow, rest, or redirect. It might not jump right out at you right away, but it's always there.

Before I found my purpose and direction, when I was being carried along the different currents I talked about in chapter three, I took pride in working for large, international corporations. It was what success looked like to me before I was intentional about defining what success meant to me. So, when a multinational food and drink processing conglomerate corporation offered me a safety management position, I did not hesitate to accept it. Granted, the position was for a small biotech company the large corporation acquired, I was happy to be part of this new and tiny subsidiary. My previous experience and skill set and the need of the organization were a perfect fit.

I thoroughly enjoyed my time there until they put me in the middle of the decision to implement certain management systems at our facility. My immediate supervisor and his supervisor resisted the management system requirements. We were not a food manufacturing or distribution facility like the other facilities that fell under the requirement. However, it was part of the corporation's internal standards, so as a subsidiary of the corporation, it was a requirement. For months I didn't know if implementing the management systems was the right thing to do. Either I would go against my supervisor and his boss (who was the COO) or I would go against the head of operations of the parent corporation. I gathered information and was prepared to implement the management systems, but I never received the approval or funding to move forward.

During this period, a recruiter from the largest international mass media and entertainment corporation reached out to me and said that they had been looking for a candidate with the combination of certifications I held. She asked if I might be interested in applying for a professional role at one of their theme parks. It was 110 miles away, a two-hour drive from our home. For that reason alone, I didn't seriously consider it. However, I agreed to review the job description and take an initial call to discuss it anyway. As tension mounted between my company and its parent corporation, the idea of working at the most famous theme park in the world sounded more and more appealing. I discussed it with my husband and tried to warm him up to the idea. It would require us to move and find another daycare and school for our kids. He was not too keen on the idea, but I started the interview process anyway. The more information I got about the position and the more tension built at my company, the more I wanted the job.

Eight months, and several phone, video, and in-person interviews later, they offered me the position. I remember the day so clearly. I had just gotten off of a call with the heads of safety for various divisions of my company. We were each asked to give a management system implementation update. When I indicated that we had not started implementation at our facility, I was scolded. I was berated and humiliated for my performance, or lack thereof, in front of the other EHS site leads. I left the office to clear my head. I remember sitting in my car in the parking lot of a busy strip mall feeling like I was at a breaking point. I called my friend Monica, sobbing, seeking consolation and advice. A few minutes into that call, I received the call from the recruiter offering me the position at the theme park. Not only were they eager for me to start, they also offered a higher salary than I expected. Under the circumstances, but reluctantly, my husband gave me his blessing to accept the position. We let the kids finish the school year where they were. They still had four months left, so I commuted almost three hours each way (after train, bus, and shuttle transfers) while we figured out our housing situation. I tried temporary housing near the theme park for a few weeks, but it was rough being away from the family during the week. In the summer, we finally moved halfway between my new job and my husband's job. My husband and I each commuted an hour-and-a-half each way in opposite directions.

Seven months later, I resigned from the position. Though I met the criteria for what they were looking for, I was not the right fit for the position. The values and the culture of the department I worked for did not resonate with mine. I told myself I would stick it out for two or three years, but there was too much friction and dissonance to cut through. I felt like a failure and disappointment to my family. My kids loved their mom working at this famous theme park. They were too young to understand why I left. We had to make so many changes for me to accept that position all to resign seven short months later. At just the right time, I was offered a great consulting position that made it easy to leave the theme park, but it still resulted in an additional four years of several hours of daily commuting for our family.

It wasn't until several years later that I was able to recognize the opportunity that came from that "mistake". The school my kids ended up at was not our first choice when we moved. We had originally planned on enrolling them in a school a few minutes away from the theme park. My coworkers discouraged me from keeping the kids closer to me than my husband. They warned that there would be long days where I might get caught up responding to incidents in the park. They said I might not get to my kids' school in time to pick them up some days. They strongly urged that if it was an option, we should send them to school somewhere near my husband's job. They painted the picture of my kids sitting on a curb waiting for two hours for my husband to drive up from his job on days I could not get off in time to pick them up. As a result, we decided to send them to school near my husband.

I was not happy that my new job determined what school my kids ended up going to. Fortunately, our initial meetings and tour at the school near my husband's company went well, and we felt good about sending them there. Fast forward a few years later, we became very involved with the parish community that our children's school was part of. We figured, we needed a new parish, we might as well attend the one affiliated with the school and take advantage of the parishioner discount. My husband and I had no idea how much of an impact the community there would have on our relationship with each other and our family. It has been a blessing to be part of this community and to grow with it. We may not have found it if it weren't for the theme park causing us to look at other alternatives. Coming to this realization took time. I went through a few years of trying to figure out why I passed through that experience. My faith was strengthened so much because of that experience. I am grateful because without it, I may not have had the courage to create and pour into the Working Moms Tribe Movement.

Reflection

Recall a time where things did not turn out as you had hoped, but eventually turned out better than what you hoped for. How long did it take and what had to happen for you to see the blessing in disguise?

CHAPTER SIX

Align Your Vibe

THE BIG WINS that result from small steps come gradually. Getting tangled is also a process that happens gradually when you're moving too quickly and without consistency and intention. By the time you start to feel the effects of being tangled, it's hard to pinpoint how you got there. Usually one or more of your four elements: vision, identity, balance, or energy, what I will refer to collectively as your V.I.B.E., has been neglected and in need of attention. It happens when life gets busy! Sometimes it doesn't take much to go from being untangled to tangled or vice versa. I remember waking up one morning ready to take on my day with my list of top three priorities in hand. I went through my morning routine, finished my coffee, and suddenly something hit me, and I lost my drive and motivation. It happened in a matter of minutes. I went from feeling pumped and focused, to sluggish and foggy. It felt like finals week during college. I could only get myself to sort, clean, and process everything else other than the things I needed to focus on. So, I did those things instead because the energy was still there, and I didn't want to waste the day. At the end of the day, I felt so discouraged and unproductive. This particular time the tangled feeling was brief, only lasting a day, but like every other time, it felt heavy and yucky! It felt like the uneasy feeling you have after interviewing for a position you really want, not knowing if your responses were good enough.

To help it pass and to get untangled, I aligned my V.I.B.E. to examine what my vision, identity, balance, and energy looked and felt like at that moment. Then I did what I could do to shift it into a gear that would get me moving forward again. I have done it enough to know what activities to try in each of the four areas. Some I can do with ease, so that's an indicator that my tangle isn't in those areas. In the areas I experience resistance, I may have to try a few things before getting to that lighter place where the clouds are moving again. It's a process you might have a tendency to forgo when things are going well. But it has its way of reminding you when it needs to be revisited and refined. It is very much like actively practicing gratitude or even taking daily vitamins. There's no question that it works and has benefits, yet we slowly let it fall through the cracks when life is good. It's not until things stop moving smoothly that we revisit these simple and vital habits we eased up on.

In the beginning, it's best to get into a rhythm of aligning your V.I.B.E. every morning. It can help you figure out what small steps you can incorporate into your morning or day to get aligned with your values, focused on your priorities, and moving. As you get used to aligning your V.I.B.E. every morning, you may not need to visit all four areas daily. You will learn which areas might have been affected by recent events and in need of special attention. I previously mentioned the importance of spending time with and focusing on yourself and being intentional about creating your plan versus allowing others around you to create your plan. Aligning your V.I.B.E. in the morning can help you prioritize your day and help you focus on how you will accomplish your priorities before other people bombard you with theirs. It will give you a moment to look at your collection of "necklaces", your unique skills and talents, and figure out which one(s) you need to "put on" to conquer the day. It can be a time to assess wins and lessons learned from the day before, let them go, or store them for future reference. If you don't already journal, it's a good practice to try to see if it's one of the habits that can help you get untangled. Aligning your V.I.B.E. routinely can help bring you back to the present to focus on today rather than the worries of the future.

Your V.I.B.E. is unique to you. What is energizing, balancing, or inspiring to you might not have the same effect on someone else. Over the next few weeks, you will get clear on:

- where you're headed
- your identities
- how to achieve and maintain a balance that works for you
- what energizes you
- what drains you

I should forewarn you that as your V.I.B.E. gets clearer and things start falling into place, you may feel compelled and confident to make drastic changes in your life. You might discover a new purpose and feel prepared to pursue the next level, explore new positions, change careers, or quit your job to pursue something completely different. You'll know it's right it if it feels a little scary but super exciting. Those are the kinds of things that happen when you're untangled.

The next few chapters will better explain each of the four elements of your V.I.B.E., and how mindfulness of them can get you untangled, freeing you to get moving again. At the highest level, your vision is how you see yourself making your impact in the world. Identity is having a clear sense of who you are, what you believe in, and what you stand for and against. Balance is how you manage your resources to process incoming information and requests. Energy is your capacity to do something you need or want to do. Vision and identity are closely tied to each other and to your dreams and goals. Balance and energy are connected and relate to your ability to work on your dreams and goals. Like any other system, when one part of the system is down or slow, the other areas will feel it and it will be apparent in overall performance. Consider your morning alignment of your V.I.B.E. your performance management system.

As a risk management professional, it's always easy to tell if an organization is proactive or reactive within the first few minutes of entering the facility or meeting with management. Proactive organizations have robust management systems in place to keep things moving efficiently and to spot opportunities for improvement quickly. They experience steady growth. Reactive organizations may experience phases of rapid growth but may have to stop or change courses often to respond to systemic issues. They often spend a lot of time and money correcting or responding to circumstances that could have been prevented, and their growth is not as steady. The same is true on the individual level. When we are not intentional about creating and managing our performance management systems, we limit our ability to grow. So next time someone asks you if you have PMS, you can take pride in responding with a "yes" for once!

Before I discovered my V.I.B.E., I was working towards the goal of an EHS Director position. I made it there, but that was when I realized it wasn't what I wanted. The organization that offered me the Director of EHS position offered it to me with a disclaimer. In more or less words, they told me I would be coming into a role that would need to interact with the heads of several other departments, and I would encounter a lot of resistance and challenging personalities. Expect very little to happen slowly, they warned. On the one hand, I appreciated the heads up. They did not sugarcoat the opportunity to make it sound more attractive than it was. On the other hand, I was given a similar forewarning at the theme park just months before. On top of that, the salary offer was $20,000 less than what I was making. I would have taken the pay cut for the right position with the right organization and the potential for growth without even thinking twice. But that was not what they were offering. The only reason I would have accepted the position is if I wanted the Director title that bad. The red flags quickly helped me to decide I did not.

Title aside, the role itself was one that I had held a few times before. I didn't care to work for another organization where I cared more about the health and safety of the employees than they did themselves. There are enough examples of safety managers facing civil and criminal penalties because they failed to protect their workers from illness or injury. In most instances, he/she genuinely tried, but still became the organization's scapegoat when the organization chose the unsafe option instead. I wasn't willing to wait for my turn to appear on that headline.

I could have waited to see what other director level opportunities came. Or I could have started exploring new but related fields. Instead, I followed a tiny whisper and veered off course. I took some time off to rest, explore, and spend time with my family. That is when I started studying the elements of the V.I.B.E. system and found clarity, increased courage and confidence, and my purpose. It felt different from any of the careers or goals I had set for myself in the past. Those were all centered around someone else's purpose. I was more than happy to use my skills and talents to help them achieve their goals when they aligned with mine and in exchange for the opportunities they gave me. When I discovered how my skills and talents could be used to change the working mom experience and to help employers make shifts to support modern family dynamics, I could not see myself going back to a career that didn't equally light me up. That would be like watering a plant that was already dead. Once you see the vision of your purpose making its impact, you can't unsee it. It will feel so scary and exciting that any other options will feel so dull compared to it. I'm excited to hear about the visions and purposes you uncover as you discover and align your V.I.B.E.

Reflection

What does your V.I.B.E. feel or look like at the moment? Do any areas stand out as needing attention?

"*Values* are the foundation of who you are, what you stand for, and what you stand against. They are the principles that tell you how to *live* your life to *achieve* what matters to you."

WORKING MOMS
TRIBE

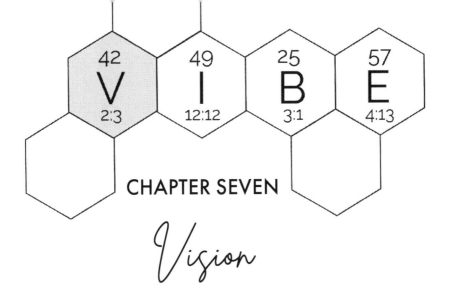

CHAPTER SEVEN

Vision

IT'S MUCH EASIER to get somewhere when you know where you're going. Though that may sound obvious, many people shy away from casting a vision to avoid making a commitment to it. It shouldn't be viewed as a commitment or obligation. It should excite and inspire you (which we'll talk more about in chapter 16). If it doesn't, you probably haven't found the right or big enough vision. That's ok, because that's what this chapter (both of this book and of your life) will be about!

Try to think back, way back before you were in a relationship, a mom, or settled on a career. You had big dreams, maybe of getting married, owning a home, having kids, owning a business, or traveling the world. Those dreams lose energy when we become moms, mostly because our energy gets shifted to taking care of the tiny humans God gifted to us. Some of us are able to find a groove and start dreaming again. While for others, it takes more time to adjust to motherhood, especially working motherhood, and our dreams get put on the back burner for much longer than they should.

In the Working Moms Tribe community, we are big on dreaming big and sharing those dreams with each other to intentionally give energy to our dreams. When we don't, it's much easier to get tangled in the requests and competing interests of everyone around us. Your dreams give clarity to your vision and your vision inspires you to set goals. Those are the steps I've broken down visioning to:

1. **Dream** big and without limits;

2. Wait for a **vision** to surface that describes the impact you would like to make in the world; and

3. Set **goals** to help you make that impact.

That's the high-level overview. Each of those steps can break down further into even smaller steps. Finding the right vision shouldn't be stressful or daunting. The approach, or even the desired outcome, can change along the way. There will always be room to adjust!

So, as you routinely align your V.I.B.E. and assess the vision element, you might evaluate your list of dreams, how you feel about your long-term vision, or set or assess your personal goals to get you closer to your vision. I keep a "small steps to big dreams" journal that describes everything the next-level version of myself does, sees, feels, hears, tastes, and smells. I get to decide who and where this next-level version of myself is. It could be me next year, in five years, or in 20 years. There is power in words and you can give energy to ideas. This practice helps with clarity and focus and programming your subconscious to act in alignment with your vision.

I am a visual learner, so visual cues help me register thoughts and ideas in my mind. I create and update a vision board regularly and place it somewhere I see regularly. Both creating it and seeing it regularly shift my energy level in positive ways. My vision board reminds me of the next-level version of myself I am actively working on and the impact I am aspiring to make. I have heard incredible testimonies of specific things from people's vision boards coming to life. I look forward to being able to share when bigger dreams on my vision board come to fruition. Africa's first woman president, Ellen Johnson Sirleaf, once said, "If your dreams don't scare you, they are not big enough." I wholeheartedly believe and adopt this. Look where it brought her! The other way I like to think about it is, there is no harm in dreaming audaciously big. If a dream on my list doesn't come true, it wasn't meant for me. I don't perceive it as a failure, and you shouldn't either! Dream bigger, in color, and without limits!

Some of the dreams on your lists will materialize through the subconscious actions and behaviors that will naturally follow. Others you will consciously materialize by intentionally setting goals to make them a reality. It might be a little scarier for you to promote a dream up to a "vision", but it's ok, a healthy dose of fear can be motivating. Usually by the time you've decided to set goals related to your vision, you've had time to think about and process the idea. Something about it must have tugged at your heart or excited you enough to move forward with it. That's when a community like Working Moms Tribe can be helpful to cheer you on and remind you that you deserve it and can achieve it.

If you don't have a clear vision of your purpose and impact, don't worry. Take a step back and start dreaming again. In the Working Moms Tribe community, we have courses that can guide you through activities that will help refine your vision. There is a short course on how to get started with your "small steps to big dreams" journal. You can do this electronically, or if you're a pen and paper girl like me, I've created a journal as a place to capture it. There is also a course that helps you to dream bigger or to start dreaming again. This can be a self-study course, but I recommend catching one of the live courses if you can. It's helpful to hear the dreams and feed off of the energy of other working moms. Once you have a clear vision, it's time to start setting goals to get there. Having a strong sense of identity, knowing who you are, helps your vision stay clear and to develop aligned goals.

Reflection

Do you have a vision of the impact your life will make? In your community, your family, the world? If you don't have one at the moment, what are the five biggest dreams you can think of for yourself (if time and money were of no concern)?

"I've learned that there is always an opportunity hidden beneath or behind adversity."

WORKING MOMS
TRIBE

"The *big wins* that result from small steps come gradually."

WORKING MOMS
TRIBE

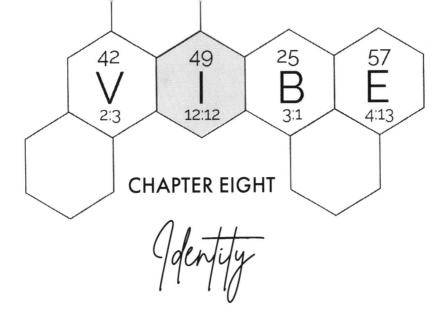

CHAPTER EIGHT

Identity

EARLIER I MENTIONED that some of your tangled necklaces represent identities (while others represent skills or experiences) you've had to assume at some point along your journey. When you're unclear on your identity, on who you are, and what you stand for, it makes it challenging to assess if your habits and behaviors are consistent with your identity. As working moms, we have multiple identities. We have our identity as mom and even within that identity we might be a single mom, military mom, special needs mom, stepmom, foster mom, adoptive mom, stay-at-home mom, work from home mom, homeschool mom, working mom, and the list goes on. We have our identity at home, in our community, in our professional life, and in our social circles. How congruent or incongruent are your LinkedIn and Facebook profiles, and was that intentional?

During the interview for the director role that I talked about in chapter six, they took me into a faculty lounge for a large panel style interview with about 20 interviewers. While we were waiting for everyone to arrive, one of the interviewers casually asked me about my ability to multi-task. I laughed and responded, "I'm a mom, I'm a pro multi-tasker." He said something like, "Cute, but seriously." I felt embarrassed for misreading the tone of the room and forgetting that I shouldn't freely offer information about things they weren't allowed to ask. I pulled my thoughts together and gave him a response more aligned with what he was looking for, "In my current role I am a project manager managing two dozen ongoing and one-time projects, I am responsible for business development to help secure enough work for my office of 13 consultants, and I am outsourced 30+ hours at one of the largest biotech companies in San Diego providing onsite technical support." I've thought about that exchange many times since. I perceived it to communicate that he did not recognize the skills I learned or sharpened as a mom as valuable. They were "cute" but there was not a place for them in a professional setting. That same year, I was told during a performance review that when I met with prospective clients, I talked too much and over shared irrelevant information. I viewed my approach as building rapport and relationship. It was the first time in 15 years that a "needs improvement" appeared on my performance evaluation. It did not sit well with me, especially considering I believed those relationship building skills were what helped me meet my lofty revenue targets for that year. Both exchanges shook me and made me second guess myself. Had I been clearer with my identities, where each was appropriate or allowed, what the expectations of the roles were, and if they conflicted with my identity, I would have handled each scenario better. Instead, I shrunk and withdrew in shame.

A woman in my prayer group asked us to pray for her because she felt her job was compromising her identity. Her faith was such a huge part of her it defined her, but she was not allowed to talk about it at work. I could see it was really weighing heavily on her heart. It sounded like her faith was a non-negotiable for her and being required to suppress it at work was affecting her. We gave her creative ways to live her faith and honor her identity without using words. We encouraged her to still pray for her co-workers who were experiencing adversity without mentioning it to them. She could also show her kindness and compassion in other ways without sharing her religious beliefs. Being clear on who you are and what you stand for helps you develop the right habits and take actions consistent with your identity. It will help you recognize when you are put in a position that might compromise your identity and how to get out of it.

Reflection

Who do you identify as? List out all your identities. Which one(s) is/are your favorite and why?

"Live out your *beliefs* when you feel you can't speak about them."

WORKING MOMS
— TRIBE —

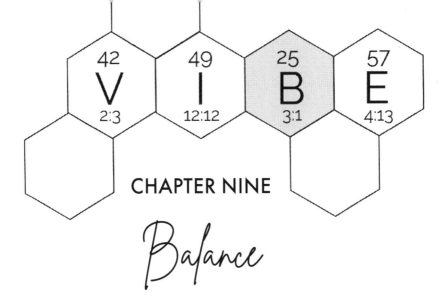

CHAPTER NINE

Balance

THE IDEA OF "balance" can be a controversial topic for working moms (or women in general). Many women don't believe balance is attainable. If you believe balance is the perfect distribution of resources to manage competing interests, I can understand why you might feel balance is unattainable. Even if you are good at planning and with time and resource management, things don't always go as planned for working moms. Additional requests can come in faster than you can adjust and cross things off the list. I don't believe balance is the perfect distribution of resources and demands, so I believe it is achievable. Recognizing the discord the term "balance" has for many people, employers and personal development professionals have coined terms like "work-life integration", "work-life sway", "work-life harmony" or "work-life blend". The words that come to mind when I think or talk about balance are "dynamic" and "recovery". There is constant adjustment and reconciliation that has to happen to restore and maintain balance. It's like chemical equations we learned about in high school and college. When things get added to either side of the equation (reactants or products), the whole system will adjust until equilibrium is achieved. Additionally, things can be added to help the system reach equilibrium faster.

Every day, you are taking small steps towards your goals and vision. In the process, those around you present you with, what I call, "asks" that are either opportunities to get you closer to your vision or threats that pull you away from your vision. The opportunities you should always take advantage of. Some of them might be scary, but if they are both scary and exciting, take a deep breath and dive in. The threats you need to be more cautious with and cognizant of. Threats require time, money, and/or energy. Before saying yes to these, determine if they are worth your investment. In assessing your daily opportunities and threats, decide which ones you will take on for the day/week, and prioritize them. In an ideal world, your opportunities would perfectly counterbalance your threats and you'd always end the day in at least a neutral position. Your net loss would be zero.

As working moms, we all know that the threats almost always outweigh the opportunities. This is another reason balance can feel so unattainable. Threats, and sometimes even opportunities, mentally, physically, emotionally, or spiritually strain and stress you. You can endure doses of strain and stress, but you need recovery between repeated doses. Tangle happens when the recovery doesn't! If you feel like the threats come faster than the opportunities and being overwhelmed doesn't ease up, it's time to get more intentional about allowing yourself to recover and counterbalance the influx of threats.

There are four main areas I categorize my recovery efforts. They are mind, heart, body, and blessings. They correlate directly and respectively to your mental, emotional, physical, and spiritual health. When aligning your V.I.B.E. and, more specifically, as you are assessing your balance, you first need to identify what causes you strain and stress. This will help you to determine where your relief and recovery efforts should be focused. As you read the next few chapters, it will help you become more aware of your mind, heart, body, and blessings and what you can do in each area to replenish and experience peace and joy. Knowing what brings you the most rest and recovery, intentionally carve in regular time and space for these practices and activities. Prime and ground yourself before (or in response to) the strain and stress. When life gets especially busy, the "asks" come in faster than you can process, and you start to feel overwhelmed, the earliest knots of tangle, do what you can to indulge in even more of these relief and recovery activities that help you most. I have observed many working moms reluctant to do this because it feels selfish to take time to rest and recover when they are needed most. I have been guilty of this myself. But I have learned that I am much more efficient and effective after rest and recovery than I am when strained or stressed. You will be too.

Mind, heart, body, and blessings are all connected and affected by each other. In the next four chapters, I will discuss each of them in more detail to help you figure out what areas of your life might need shifting and recovery to feel balanced. They will also give ideas on the types of practices and activities that can aid in recovery and therefore balance. Some recovery exercises that work in one area can help to improve multiple areas. Try not to get too concerned with categorizing recovery efforts into only one category. The important thing is to experience recovery, and therefore balance, regularly. The second half of this book will discuss general ideas such as who you surround yourself with, developing the right mindset, staying focused, overcoming fear and adversity, and being authentic. I had originally attempted to associate each chapter with one of the four V.I.B.E. elements then with one of the four areas of balance. Where they will be most applicable and helpful for you will be highly dependent on your situation and experiences. I ended up taking a different approach, leaving it open for you to apply each topic to the area(s) of your life that need it most. Please note, I am not a medical professional. Information covered in this book is not intended to be used as a substitute for consultation with a licensed medical professional. If you feel you are experiencing illness or injury, please seek professional help.

Reflection

Do you feel balance is achievable? Why or why not? Does framing it as "an act of recovery" and recognizing that it is very fluid change your response?

"You can do *magical* things when you're inspired, and *inspiration* can be found everywhere!"

WORKING MOMS
—— TRIBE ——

"One of the unique benefits of being a mom is a never-ending supply of *inspiration* in our children."

CHAPTER TEN

Balance Through Mind

YOUR MIND IS the part of your body that receives information from all around you, processes that information, and tells your body how to respond. Decisions, thoughts, feelings, ideas, and actions all start in your mind. If you are not intentional, daily opportunities and threats that compete for your attention and energy will consume your mind. They will out-compete the clarity and capacity needed to process information in a way that promotes growth, progress, and your values. It's like a cluttered desk or workspace. When it's disorganized and filled with too much stuff, it makes it hard to find things you need or to get any work done. Clearing and organizing your desk or workspace is necessary to keep the space useful and functional. Your mind also needs to be free and clear enough to process incoming information into meaningful output. You might feel tangled when you process too much information, draining your energy, but don't feel any closer to your purpose or vision. This can happen when you spend so much energy on other people's priorities and not your own. If this is one of the areas you identify as needing attention, track what makes you feel strained and stressed, try different exercises that help with prioritizing and protecting your time and energy, and be intentional about focusing on your priorities either before or in addition to others'. Focus on the objective of getting more efficient at receiving and processing information so you won't feel resentful that others' needs are being met at the expense of yours.

There are lots of ways to promote mental health to keep your mind clear and ready to orchestrate the right responses. Find the habits that will make it easy to start with a fresh slate, create your list, prioritize, decide, and act. Clearing your slate will comprise activities from all four recovery areas (mind, heart, body, and blessings). Find a morning or nightly routine that helps you to exhale, decompress, and relieve tension. Then you can create and prioritize your to-do list for the day or week ahead. Each new day will bring new opportunities and threats, which will then need to be weighed and assessed against your prioritized to-do list. In a perfect world there'd be some overlap, and that would make it easier to get through it all. In the real world, you have to pick and choose what makes the list, what gets checked off the list, and what falls off the list. When you try to do it all without prioritizing, what's important to you might inadvertently fall off the list. So far, a combination of a paper planner, a reusable notebook that stores the pages electronically, and occasionally a to-do app on my phone, are where and how I prioritize my tasks and goals. What works best for you might be all digital. Go with whatever gives you the best results. Then move on to deciding what has to happen to cross things off the list and take action.

Your ability to confidently make decisions is critical to your mental health. It can be tempting to put off what seem like small decisions. But remember, the small steps are what lead up to the big wins. When you delay those small steps, you are also delaying the downstream activities. My messy house is a reminder of this. Sometimes when we introduce new things into our home, we don't decide where their designated spots will be. Or when we check the mail, we don't decide what needs to happen with each piece and end up with piles of paper of indecision. Indecision is a sure way to get tangled. When you are able to make the small decisions but choose not to, you are allowing small jams to turn into clutter or bigger jams. If we can avoid those (and we sure can) we should. Make the small decisions and do what needs to be done to follow through. Clear the clutter to make room for the big decisions. Making those small, easy decisions is also good practice for making the bigger, more critical decisions.

The "big decisions" are the ones that come with bigger risks and, more often than not, paralyzing fear. There are things you can do to lower the risk, but it's rare to be able to eliminate it completely. When you can't lower it to an acceptable level, you may retreat or delay to avoid making a decision. Sometimes the decision will get made for you, sometimes you'll get the information you need to make the decision, and sometimes you'll be backed into a corner and forced to decide. The approach I take for big decisions is the same approach I take with everything else; break them down into smaller decisions, don't get too tied to particular outcomes, and be ready and willing to adjust, if needed.

I caught myself doing it with my daughter with a small for me, but big for her, decision. When I began working for myself and from home, I had to make a lot of shifts to get productive. One thing I tried, and that has been working well, is putting on makeup and getting dressed every morning as if I still worked in an office or at a client site. My daughter, who was not yet in preschool, had been home with me during this time, so when she woke up every morning, she saw me dressed up and ready (usually with nowhere to go), and thought it was normal. For us, in this season, it is! She greeted me with a big "Good morning!", immediately followed with, "I want to wear a pretty dress." If she's anything like my older daughter, she will soon hate dresses. Until then, we'll continue with our dress up routine in the mornings. Sometimes she will know exactly which dress or look she wants. For example, one day she was fixed on dressing like a ballerina. She watched something the night before, so she knew she wanted her hair in a tight, clean bun with a tiara, a soft pink tutu, and ballerina slippers. Other days she has trouble deciding what to wear, so I help her with her decision. I start by asking her to pick a color. Next, I have her decide, pants or dress. Eventually, after a series of a few choices, she'll have the perfect outfit picked out. It may not match, and it might be inside out and backwards, but it always works and can be changed if it doesn't! I do the same with my bigger life decisions.

When recruiters used to reach out to me on LinkedIn with job opportunities, I'd start by asking myself if I was even open to a new job. If it wasn't an obvious yes or no, I'd ask for the job description or take a call to learn more about the position. Then I would decide if I would submit my resume or apply. Then I decided if I would take the interview or not. I broke down the process into several steps, leaving the opportunity to change direction at any point of the process if needed. Sometimes my mind would jump too far ahead in the process and start thinking about if and how I would resign or negotiating my salary even before they even offered the job to me. I'd have to remind myself to cross each bridge as it came and to be ok if things turned out differently from what I envisioned. On that note, I applied and took job interviews often. I viewed it as part of the process of gathering the information I needed to make my decision. The information from each step is what would determine if I took the next step in the process or not.

The last part of the information processing sequence is taking action, another step with high potential for getting tangled! Working moms have lots of explanations for not taking action, some are valid, which we'll call "reasons", while others are not, which we'll call "excuses". You might be tired, in which case finding balance, or recovery might be the solution. Or you might be scared, we'll address that in the fear less chapter. Getting to the root of why you're not taking action can definitely help to process things off your list, get untangled, and get things moving again. If you're having trouble with either your list of priorities or your choices of action to take, try a brain dump. Write or type out every single thought running through your mind as it comes, no matter how small or complex. Keep on writing until nothing else comes to mind. As you review what you wrote, it should get easier to group and categorize ideas and actions. You can process thoughts or ideas that have been in the back of your mind and decide they are a "no" and cross them off the list. That is already a small action that helps to process some of the thoughts and information that might have been cluttering your mind. For what's left on your list, decide if you'll tackle the "easy actions" or the ones that will have the most impact on your life. If you choose the latter, you might have to break down each thought or idea into a series of actions that need to happen to complete each task. Remember, some of the practices and activities from the other areas of recovery (heart, body, and blessings) might be what get your mind untangled. Try whatever resonates with you and slowly develop habits out of the ones that work and give you favorable results. Remember, start small. Small steps lead to big wins.

Reflection

What activities do you engage in (or will you try) to clear your mind and improve your mental health?

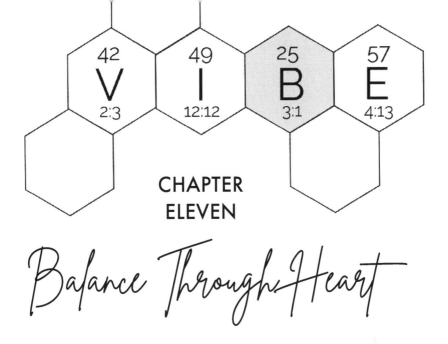

CHAPTER
ELEVEN

Balance Through Heart

THE MIND AND heart function so closely together that it's hard to separate the information and thoughts in your mind from the feelings and emotions in your heart. As animals, we are programmed to quickly process information from our environment, decide if it's a threat or opportunity, and respond appropriately. We usually make the determination in seconds and respond with either fear and defense or excitement and anticipation. As humans, we experience a wider range of feelings and emotions in response to the information we receive from our environment. As moms, our kids help ensure we experience the full spectrum of feelings and emotions every day! You could wake up early Monday morning to get ahead of your week by starting with yoga, meditation, and a fresh cup of coffee, feeling energized, prepared, and motivated. Then it comes time to get the kids up and ready for school and in minutes the house could be overtaken by yelling, tension, and stress. Feelings of defeat can quickly take over before you've even left the house. Running late, you snap and lose it over your kid(s) not putting their shoes on and getting in the car. You drop off or see them off, feeling guilty for yelling at them over their shoes, but the guilt is quickly overshadowed by the apprehension of having to walk into work late. It doesn't take much to take you from feeling blessed to feeling stressed. But the opposite is also true!

You may have heard the idiom, "don't cry over spilled milk." I have definitely cried over spilled milk. Whether it was breast milk I poured into a bottle that I forgot to put a liner into, or the milk my daughter poured on the floor instead of her bowl of cereal as she tried to aim and pour the heavy bottle of milk by herself. I did not control my response and have literally cried over spilled milk. There was a time in my life where moments like these were common. I would succumb to the pressure of the "threats" waiting in my email inbox or at work, responding irrationally. I have since learned how to pause, take a deep breath, and redirect the course of the day or week. It is now rare for my first response to be yelling, door slamming, or road rage. I now choose to come from the heart, accept the curveballs that are just a part of life, brush it off, and proceed with my day or week. It takes time to shift from letting your mind control your heart to thinking from your heart. As you do it more consciously, the difference in results will positively reinforce the behavior and it should help to avoid some knots and tension that ultimately lead to getting tangled.

Training yourself to be able to see things from various perspectives is a good way to get into the habit of thinking with your heart. Daniel Goleman has published several influential books on the value of emotional intelligence. Emotional intelligence involves learning how to recognize and work with your emotions and the emotions of those around you to achieve specific outcomes. Empathy, or the ability to put yourself in someone else's shoes, is one of the key components of emotional intelligence. Practicing empathy is a good way for you to learn how to look at things from another point of view, or perspective. Anyone that has ever had their car or home broken into, knows how furious, hurt, scared, or violated it feels to discover the door ajar and stuff rifled through and missing. It is a huge inconvenience to clean up the mess, figure out what they took and what else is at risk, and potentially file an insurance claim. It would be natural to respond by yelling and cursing, to take it out on the next person you encounter, and to allow it to ruin the rest of your day. You might beat yourself up about where you parked, why you left valuables in the car, or if you might have left the door unlocked. Alternatively, you could change your perspective and think about why someone might have done it. Maybe the person was a runaway or homeless and in need of the clothes in your gym bag. Or maybe he or she was desperate for money and needed to sell the laptop that was left in the car. Changing your perspective won't make the situation any less inconvenient, but it can help with how you respond, and protect your heart and energy.

I used to try to seek out and surround myself with like-minded people until I heard someone explain why he would prefer to surround himself with like-hearted people. It made me pause and reflect on the ideal qualities of the people I want and should allow into my circle. Yes, it is ideal to be around people who share the same opinions and preferences as we do. However, I would much rather be surrounded and influenced by those who share the same values as I do, those who would respond from the same heart as I would.

Protecting and strengthening the heart to better manage feelings and emotions is a better investment of time and energy compared to finding ways to recover. But we do need both skill sets to stabilize the emotional roller coaster we got on when we became working moms. This is probably the area of balance that will get challenged the most. This means it presents the most opportunities to try out and practice new things to better process your feelings and emotions. When breaking this one down to the small steps, the triggering circumstance, the feeling, and the response can all be separated out with awareness and discipline. You can and should always acknowledge your feelings and allow yourself to process them, but put thought into which ones just need to pass and an appropriate response for those that warrant one. The second half of the book will help with developing skills to do this.

Reflection

Think of a recent incident that could have turned out differently had you paused and changed your perspective before responding?

"Tangle happens when the *recovery* doesn't!"

WORKING MOMS
TRIBE

"There is constant *adjustment* and *reconciliation* that has to happen to restore and maintain *balance*."

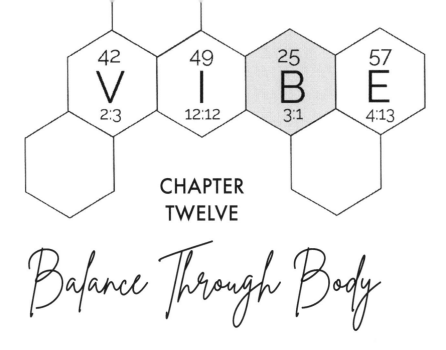

CHAPTER
TWELVE

Balance Through Body

WHEN THE EXTERNAL "asks" become too stressful, many of us can find relief, recovery, and balance through diet, exercise, and sleep. There is a lot of focus on these areas when discussing care of the body and physical health. Growing up I was taught the importance of eating enough of each of the basic food groups, getting at least eight hours of sleep each night, and exercise. As someone who studied biochemistry in college, I learned about the metabolic pathways in the body and how they are affected by proper diet, exercise, and sleep. There is no doubt these are essential as we care for our bodies and physical health and there are tons of resources available to help you set and achieve your goals. What is not talked about or valued enough is the body of the working mom as the vessel that grew and birthed tiny humans and all the stress it experiences as it fulfills the needs of our careers and our families.

I am often asked why I support and created a community for working moms and not all working parents. One of the reasons is that working moms experience unique challenges that working dads do not experience. Among these are the physical needs and changes associated with getting pregnant, nursing, and the months (possibly years) of recovery following delivery. These are on top of trying to keep up with diet, exercise, and sleep. I wanted to create a community where it was safe to support, address, and talk about challenges like these and how they affect and overlap with our ability to recover and find balance. Not too long ago, I participated in a discussion of moms sharing ideas to balance work and motherhood. One mom shared how she felt like her body was no longer hers. Her breastfeeding baby constantly demanded the top half of her body and her husband constantly demanded the bottom half. It was the perfect example of something experienced by a working mom that a working dad or a woman without children would never understand.

When I got pregnant the first time, I worked on a laboratory bench developing nucleic acid-based diagnostic assays. I sometimes worked with chemicals that were harmful to a developing fetus, so I disclosed my pregnancy to my employer immediately to avoid working with or around those chemicals. I worked in the biotech industry for many years and observed many pregnant women both knowingly and unknowingly working with and around such chemicals, taking the risk of exposing their developing fetuses to chemicals specifically harmful to developing fetuses. They did not feel comfortable disclosing their pregnancies that early. One in four women experiences a miscarriage. That is just one of many reasons women do not want to disclose their pregnancy too early. Miscarriage and infertility are other physical, mental, and emotional health challenges unique to women. These are very private experiences women can't or won't openly discuss but are still addressing, even if no one else knows about it.

Having passed through the child-bearing years, I have learned about so many conditions working moms might silently experience, endure, and recover from before, during, and after pregnancy. Endometriosis, polycystic ovary syndrome (PCOS), ectopic pregnancy, morning sickness, incompetent cervix, various placental and amniotic fluid conditions, pruritic urticarial papules, and plaques of pregnancy (PUPPP), gestational diabetes, anemia, abnormal hormone levels, genetic disorders, excessive bleeding, and reproductive organ abnormalities. These are just some of them but there are so many more that I have never even heard of or learned about yet. The changes to my body and conditions I experienced after the birth of each of my children were different each time and dictated my recovery and bonding experiences. I tore and experienced a lot of swelling after my first baby. I could not even sit comfortably for at least six weeks after giving birth. It took me about four months to get used to breastfeeding and it was painful. I remember laying on the floor in pain with mastitis a few days after giving birth to my third baby. It felt like a terrible flu on top of the breast hardness and pain. I remember having to leave work early one day because of clogged milk ducts and a recurrence of mastitis during that same postpartum recovery. I lost a significant amount of hair about four months after having each of my babies, but the amount I lost after my fourth baby was noticeably more. I remember being very self-conscious about the patches of thin or no hair framing my face and the short spikey hair as it slowly grew back several years (not months this time) after giving birth.

As women, we experience so many more challenges and conditions inside and outside of the body that require additional recovery and consideration. In addition to our diet, exercise, and sleep behaviors and activities, we also have to consider monthly self-breast checks, periodic pap-smears, mammograms, and menstruation and menopause abnormalities. As painful, uncomfortable, and embarrassing treatment and care in these areas can be, they are critical to our overall physical health, ability to recover and find balance, and our ability to effectively manage our opportunities and threats.

Always listen to your body! Your body was created with very elaborate and sophisticated systems that send you signs and signals to let you know what it needs or if something is not right. These signs and signals should always get moved to the top of your priorities as soon as you become aware of them. Be mindful of the levels of pain and discomfort you allow your body to experience. Moderate levels can be expected at the end of a day or week. However, if you find that you are not recovering from the pain or discomfort shortly after, it may be an indicator the stress you are being exposed to is excessive. Left unchecked or uncorrected, the pain or discomfort will result in illness or injury. In the workplace, I have investigated too many workplace injuries that were a result of workers disregarding and pushing through the pain of repetitive motion, excessive stress, or poor workstation setup. No job is worth risking injury, illness, loss of physical function, and a lower quality of life at home. Be gentle with your body, know its limits, and listen to it when it's trying to tell you what it needs. It is a gift and vessel to live out your purpose. It should be treated as such.

Reflection

What is your body telling you it needs. What is your plan to address it?

"Make the small *decisions* and do what needs to be done to *follow through*."

WORKING MOMS
TRIBE

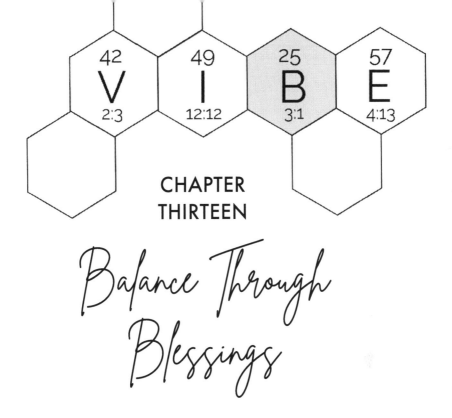

CHAPTER
THIRTEEN

Balance Through Blessings

BLESSINGS, THE TERM I prefer to use for spiritual health, relates to the belief that something bigger than you, beyond your body and physical surroundings, guides and governs your life. Being able to put faith and trust into something or someone your human senses can't detect can be strange if it's new to you. It can also foster a sense of comfort and relief. To have someone or something to transfer your fear, anxiety, or worry to, to guide you through moments of fear and uncertainty can be reassuring, uplifting, and freeing.

I have put my faith in God, and it has had the most profound effect on my ability to find balance. For this reason, I am extremely intentional about starting my morning routine with prayer. Sometimes, I wake up with thoughts already racing through my mind and I am anxious to get to my to-do list. On mornings like this, I may need to meditate or do breathing exercises before or during my prayer time to calm my nerves and focus my attention. Quality prayer time helps me feel confident and ready to start my day. When I wake up late and attempt to dive into my day without prayer or even a brief aligning of my V.I.B.E., I definitely notice a difference in the quality of my day. It feels very scattered, one thing blends into the next, and I run a high risk of getting tangled. Staying connected to God, trusting his plan for me, and paying attention to how my prayers are being answered have been a saving grace for me as a working mom.

The numbers in the graphic on the V.I.B.E. title pages represent my favorite bible scriptures related to V.I.B.E. in case you were curious.

There are other "higher powers" that working moms put their faith in. When managing your opportunities and your threats, looking for the signs and messages your higher power sends you on what to do next can take the pressure off you to figure it all out. They are everywhere! I do not believe in coincidences because of how many times I have experienced the perfect answer to my prayer come at just the right moment. I am still human and have moments of fear, worry, and doubt. My faith, like other skills and habits, takes time and practice and gets strengthened when put to the test. The answers don't always look like what I hope or ask for, but they are always perfect. It may take time to see and understand, but when it becomes clear, it is beautiful and brings peace.

Seeking holy or divine moments is much like having an attitude of gratitude. It's the recognition of the positive things happening in your life. As you actively seek them, you also invite and attract more positive things and moments into your life. My faith is so strong because I have continually experienced so many holy and divine moments. It would be remiss of me to deny or discredit them. Some are subtle while others are so blatant. One that I will never be able to shake off is how God and guardian angels spared my younger daughter's life when she was two years old. We were in my bedroom and I had just recorded a video of an outfit she had picked out and put on. She was so proud of her gray t-shirt with colorful sequin hearts and soft pink tutu. Both pieces were three sizes too big for her because they were her older sister's old clothes. She finished off the look with a hot pink and white headband with flowers and posed and twirled for me as I recorded the video. About a minute later, a large dresser tipped and toppled on her. I was two feet away, but I was looking down at my phone reviewing the video I had just recorded of her. She must have opened too many drawers, and it was not bolted or bracketed. It was the most terrifying minute of my life. I was sure it had crushed her. My adrenaline kicked in and I jumped up to lift the heavy dresser up and off of her. I had to yell to my husband and son to come lift it back into place as I was able to lift it just enough to see her. I was not expecting her to be able to move. But as soon as I lifted the dresser, she started to cry and stood up. I was scared to touch her because I didn't know if and where she might be hurt or injured. As she started to walk and move, I hugged her and began to examine her. Not a single bump, bruise, or scratch on her body. I immediately called the hospital, and they gave me instructions to monitor at home. I've told this story dozens of times, but unless you were there and heard and saw the crash of the heavy dresser, it's difficult to understand how much of a miracle it was. Blessings like these are what assure me I am not doing this life alone. They sustain me when life feels like too much to manage.

If your blessings or spiritual health involve religion like mine does, it can be a challenge. It can make those around you uncomfortable if they don't share the same belief(s) and because it's not a topic that is welcomed in the workplace. As wise Abe Lincoln once said, "Actions speak louder than words." Live out your beliefs when you feel you can't speak about them. Staying aligned with your beliefs will help you get or stay untangled. There are many ways to creatively incorporate your spiritual practices into your day. Or you may prefer to do it in private. Remember, the components you use to find balance will be unique and personal to you. No one gets to tell you what's right or wrong for you. They are not managing the same opportunities and threats as you are, so they don't get a say in how you manage or counterbalance them!

Reflection

What or who do you believe to be responsible for the blessings in your life. Is this a significant source of recovery and balance for you?

"The *mind and heart* function so closely together that it's hard to separate the information and thoughts in your mind from the *feelings and emotions* in your heart."

WORKING MOMS
TRIBE

"The approach I take for *big* decisions is the same approach I take with everything else; break them down into *smaller* decisions, don't get too tied to particular outcomes, and be ready and willing to *adjust*, if needed."

WORKING MOMS
TRIBE

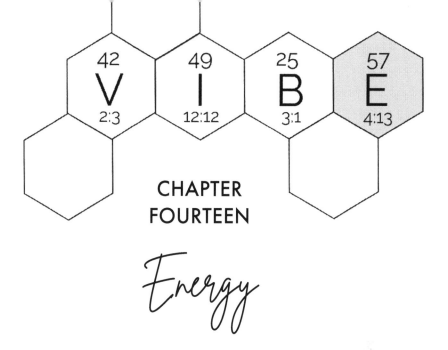

42	49	25	57
V	I	B	E
2:3	12:12	3:1	4:13

CHAPTER
FOURTEEN

Energy

ENERGY IS THE ability to do work. As implied by your title, a "working mom" needs energy. People, places, and things all carry a distinct energy. Energy is characterized by the frequency people, places, or things vibrate. When you are feeling light and positive, you are experiencing a high vibrational frequency. When you are feeling low, dark, and heavy you are experiencing a low vibrational frequency. The vibrational frequencies of people, places, and things around you affect your vibrational energy state. If you've ever experienced days where you just don't want to get out of bed in the morning or do anything, your vibrational energy level is probably really low in those moments. Having this awareness can help you find what's needed to shift your energy to get back into a state of being able to work and function again. It's an important part of getting untangled.

It's equally important to learn how to protect your energy when it's at optimal levels! As you develop your routine of aligning your V.I.B.E., you will become more aware of what positively and negatively shifts your energy. I am very in tune with how my energy changes with different people and experiences. Sometimes I can feel my energy go down as soon as someone enters a room! Lately I have been very intentional about who I spend time with and allow into my circle of influence. I am mindful to not allow negative energy in. As a working mom, energy is a precious resource, so we can't allow people who aren't intentional about protecting their energy to lower ours. Similarly, I can feel my vibrational energy level shift with positive or negative experiences. Even the thought of positive experiences has the power to raise my vibrational energy. So, I seek out positive experiences and browse through old photos often to revisit previous positive experiences.

It used to surprise me when some of my most outgoing, energetic friends would share that they were introverts. It wasn't until I learned that being an extrovert or introvert was more about where you draw your energy, that I understood. I draw my energy from the energy of people in the room. I enjoy meeting as many new people as I can and sharing thoughts, ideas, and energy with them. People recharge me. I am without a doubt, an extrovert. My introverted friends draw their energy from time with themselves or one-to-one interactions. They get drained when spending time around many people and it takes a lot of mental preparation for them to attend large events. They recharge in solitude. Knowing both where you draw your energy and how to protect and recharge it is necessary to ensuring you always have enough of it.

In his book *Think Like a Monk*, former monk turned Purpose Coach, Jay Shetty talks about how you can start your day on a positive note by being intentional with the sights, sounds, and scents you wake up to in the morning. You can increase the vibrational energy of your bedroom by placing positive imagery where you will see it when you wake up or by looking out the window to enjoy things in nature. You can influence the sounds by setting your sound system or phone to play specific music or sounds from nature to wake you. You can diffuse essential oils, light a candle, or sniff fresh flowers to start your morning with uplifting scents. The aroma of fresh coffee is the scent of choice of many working moms! Conversely, starting your day by checking your phone to read text messages, emails, or news stories is likely to decrease your vibrational energy.

Knowing your capacity and setting healthy boundaries are excellent ways to protect your energy. If you journal as part of aligning your V.I.B.E, be sure to keep track of the things that raise your energy level so you can be intentional about doing more of those things to stay positive, increase your capacity, and energize others around you. Only give your time to what raises your vibrational energy and avoid what lowers it. Don't be afraid to say no if it will cost you energy you cannot afford to give up. Do not waste energy on people who do not deserve it. Your vision, identity, balance, and energy are all interrelated. When there is a problem with one of the elements, the whole system slows or stops, and things get tangled. Aligning your V.I.B.E. regularly and finding the habits that make each element shine are your key to achieving the confidence, courage, and clarity you need to get or stay untangled.

Reflection

On a loose sheet of paper write down any negative thoughts consuming your energy at this moment. It can be a person, experience, incident, or memory. Write a note of forgiveness or release for each, tear it up, and discard it. In your planner or journal, or on a whiteboard or mirror, write down any positive thoughts that make you happy or bring you joy. They might be bible scriptures, inspirational quotes, or words of affirmation. Refer to them when you need to raise your vibrational energy.

CHAPTER FIFTEEN

Mindset Over Matter

IN THE FIRST half of the book, we established that you're not stuck, you're not lost, and you're not a hot mess. The opportunities and threats of life can make it hard to keep track of skills, identities, and experiences that you've collected along your journey, so you may have gotten tangled. I introduced how you can align your V.I.B.E. (vision, identity, balance, and energy) regularly to help you get untangled. I broke it down into small steps to encourage you to start trying whatever resonates with you. The next half of the book will talk about more ways to get untangled by exploring the elements of your V.I.B.E. deeper to learn which ones you might personally need to focus on. The experiences and ideas I share may strike you as being more relevant to one of the V.I.B.E. elements than the others. It will depend largely on where you are in your journey. Regardless of where you are, you'll need the right mindset to get to wherever you're trying to go and to ensure you don't give up before you get there.

One of my favorite books is Rachel Hollis' *Girl Wash Your Face*. It calls out the limiting beliefs (the lies) that have kept women from becoming who they were meant to be. It empowers readers to overcome the lies and adopt the right beliefs and attitudes, or mindset, to live the lives they were meant to live. It's a great read if your mindset has gotten in the way of your progress or success.

Your mindset is how you feel about your ability to achieve or accomplish something and your worthiness of it. Some people believe they were given limited abilities, or they are not worthy to achieve their goals, dreams, or vision. Other people believe they have the power to learn or develop the skills and abilities they need to accomplish whatever they set their mind to. This is the difference between those that consistently hit their goals and targets, those that don't, and those that don't even try. Those who genuinely believe they CAN will DO whatever they need to, even when they encounter a setback or adversity. They use it as an opportunity to learn the skill(s) they need to get them there. They embody a can-do attitude.

Developing the right mindset requires you to take an honest look at your beliefs in yourself, your abilities, and what you believe you deserve. You might have to think back on how each belief formed and to reshape your beliefs based on what you know to be true now. I used to have a scarcity mindset. I would only buy things on sale or clearance because I was afraid I was going to run out of money. Then I wouldn't enjoy, let alone use, a lot of the stuff I bought to preserve it and keep it new and nice for as long as possible. There would be clothes with tags in my closet that went out of style before I used them. They would get donated with their tags, never worn or enjoyed. I did not use to volunteer my time as freely unless I felt I had something to gain by doing so. When I thought about where I developed this mindset, I realized it was because I am the daughter of immigrants. My parents were both born in the Philippines and migrated to the United States when my dad joined the U.S. Navy in the early 1970s. By the time I was born, they were pretty assimilated to their new way of life, but they held onto a lot of the beliefs and practices from the Philippines. Some of those, particularly those around money, transferred to me and my siblings.

We were not poor when I was a child, but the money that came in was all accounted for and limited. My parents' language and behaviors reflected that, and it is what was engrained in us. I was the designated coupon cutter and organizer, and we would only buy groceries on the military base with the coupons I cut. We would buy two-liter bottles of sodas, but they were stored in the garage and could only be opened when we had guests. We were allowed to buy one new outfit for Christmas and one for Easter, the rest of our clothes were our school uniforms or gifts. We were scolded if a light was left on in an unoccupied room. As long as something was still working, could still be eaten, or could (in theory) be used again, it would not get thrown away. I kid you not, there is a yellow 1970s cooking range in my mom's garage that has been there for decades because "it still works". If it was small enough to box and ship, it would be sent to her siblings in the Philippines. There was always a large box in our living room or garage accumulating items that would be sent to my cousins in the Philippines. It wasn't until I went to visit them in the Philippines as a teenager that I understood what shaped my parents' habits and behaviors. They grew up poor, as did a majority of the country. They didn't take anything for granted and valued everything they worked hard to buy. They knew, all too well, what it was like to live without, so they would store more than we needed to ensure we would never experience that life. I was not properly taught how to save, invest, or manage money because most of what came in went right back out to cover expenses, aside from meager savings. My parents never passed up an opportunity to remind us "we're not rich", nor did they ever give us reason to believe we might be one day.

My dad died when I was 11 years old, leaving my mom to raise the four of us solo. I watched my dad's death both break her down and build her up into the strong, single mom she needed to be. When I was in high school, my mom fell into severe depression and admitted herself into the hospital for proper treatment. Not long after she returned home, she quit her job, presumably because of stress. That year, I remember asking her when we were going to go buy my Christmas dress. She explained she couldn't afford new clothes that year, so I would have to wear something I already had. Being the hormonal teenager I was, I did not accept that response. I locked myself in my room in anger. She knocked on my door, trying to explain our situation to me, but I wasn't hearing it. Then she started to pull out newer, or at least outfits that still had tags on them, from her closet and offer them to me. I declined them and stayed in my room and cried instead, hoping it would make her feel bad enough to take me to the mall. She did not.

I was not an easy teenager. I got straight A's, so I believed it entitled me things. I recall staying up late and disregarding my mom's phone curfew regularly. One night she had enough of me disrespecting her rules. She told me to get in the car, drove, and attempted to drop me off at juvenile hall. They would not take me because I had not committed a crime. They recommended she take me to the YWCA. I didn't know what that meant. She gave me an ultimatum. Either I respect her rules, or she'd bring me to YWCA to live somewhere I might learn to appreciate her home. She was not messing around. Her message registered, so I did my best to follow the rules.

After taking time for herself, and taking classes to become a paralegal, she found a new job and a new career with the Veteran's Administration (VA). She went back to school to get a master's degree while working full time. At one point she, my sister, my twin brother, and I were all in college at the same time. It helped us all qualify for financial aid. My first year at UCLA, I experienced culture shock and homesickness. I begged my mom to come home and she would not allow it. I told her I could save money and go to a junior college near home instead. She reminded me how blessed I was to have been accepted and to have the opportunity. I reluctantly agreed to stay. She finished her master's degree in vocational rehabilitation the year before I graduated from college. It helped her to get promoted and qualify for better positions with the VA where she helped veterans understand, obtain, and use the benefits they were entitled to.

I learned so much from watching my mom after my dad died. I learned the importance of education, to never stop learning, and that it was ok to try different things until you find the right calling. I learned that when you experience adversity, it's ok to allow yourself time to heal and recover, but you get back up and keep moving. I learned to pray and trust God from her. I experienced a mother's unconditional and tough love for her child. I am a strong, confident woman because of her. I believe I can do whatever I put my mind to because of her.

Despite all these things, I have moments of doubt. To overcome it, I immerse myself in positive affirmations, motivational and inspirational quotes, and bible scriptures. I surround myself with people with positive attitudes who inspire me to be better. I take advantage of every opportunity to learn more. I do these things to maintain growth and abundance mindsets. I intentionally practice an attitude of gratitude, focusing on how much I have, knowing it is enough. Other mindsets I know I've adopted along the way are "get-it -done" and "no excuses" mindsets. I believe these will all help me get closer to my vision. I also believe that I will experience and learn more along the way and that it will be beautiful. No matter where you are going, there is a mindset to get you there.

Reflection

Is there a mindset that you either know you'd like to let go or one that you know you need to develop? What do you believe you deserve and is possible for you?

"Being able to put *faith and trust* into something or someone your human senses can't detect can be strange if it's new to you. It can also foster a sense of *comfort and relief*."

CHAPTER SIXTEEN

Inspiration

YOU CAN DO magical things when you're inspired, and inspiration can be found everywhere! So why aren't we all sprinkling glitter everywhere, freezing time, turning things into maids, personal chefs, and trees that grow money? That's what I thought to myself as I was trying to gather my thoughts to write this book. I had my vision, and I made writing this book one of my goals to help get me to the version of myself in my vision. But every time I sat down to write it, the right thoughts and words didn't come. I had too many other things running through my head, blocking the inspiration from coming through to do its magical thing. It's when I learned how delicate, yet powerful inspiration is, why it's so important to be aware of what fosters it and blocks it, and how to harness it.

I've heard other moms say their best inspiration comes in the shower. They must have a bathroom door and a lock, without little ones who let themselves in as they please! I found that my best inspiration comes to me when I'm driving longer distances and late at night when I'm lying in the dark, just about ready to fall asleep. Sometimes, the thought or idea is so great, I have to grab my phone and write myself a note, so I won't forget it in the morning. Other times I found myself feeling inspired to write chapters in this book was whenever I was having a talk with one of my kids, trying to break down a life lesson into terms a child could understand. It comes anytime you can successfully still your brain and quiet the other thoughts running through your head, not a simple task for a working mom! Our minds are always thinking about the list of things that need to get done. If not that, it's dwelling on something that strikes the mom guilt chord. It's never-ending! But now and then, sometimes with a cup of soothing tea, intentional quiet time, a nature walk, or a song, we can clear our heads just enough to let the inspiration in.

This is a good place to distinguish between motivation and inspiration, words that are often used interchangeably, but they are not the same. Motivation is more of a, "if you do this, then you will be rewarded with that" drive. Whereas inspiration is a force that stimulates you from within to get up and do something, usually creative or to benefit people around you. I perceive motivation as tied to incentives, and inspiration coming from the heart. More simply put, motivation is an external force and inspiration is an internal drive. It was important for me to distinguish inspiration from motivation so that you can be more aware of what's moving you and intentional about seeking it out. Motivation is definitely a good thing to have, but it is more relevant when trying to restore or maintain balance. As a working mom, it's a useful skill to know how to both motivate and inspire those around you to influence behaviors both at home and at work.

Doing things borne from inspiration counterbalance things you perceive as obligations. It's important for your spirit and your vision. Your vision is a lifelong plan. You will undoubtedly need regular doses of inspiration to get you moving to take the small actions that will get you there. You won't feel inspired every day, but you can still strive to find it wherever and whenever you can and turn it into progress, whether tiny or massive.

One of the unique benefits of being a mom is a never-ending supply of inspiration in our children. Yes, they exhaust you, but they also give you reasons to try harder and do better. They may disappoint you as they learn, but they also make you proud as they accomplish new things. Never forget about or overlook the inspiration that can be found in your child(ren)! It is far more powerful than inspiration that can be drawn from anything else.

With practice and intention, you will get better and better at finding and harnessing inspiration. In your moments of inspiration, amplify them by being a source of inspiration to others. You will be pleasantly surprised what this does for both your vision and theirs!

Reflection

Write down the people, places, things, or activities you know to be inspiring for you? What are things you would like to do, see, experience, or try, to support your dreams, vision, or goals?

"You'll know it's *right* it if it feels a little scary but super *exciting*."

WORKING MOMS
TRIBE

CHAPTER SEVENTEEN

Alignment

AS AN EHS professional, performing ergonomic evaluations on employee workstations was a routine request. Our goal was to make sure employees knew how to properly adjust their workstations to their bodies. Usually, employees try to adjust their bodies to accommodate their workstation and/or equipment, and that's when they would begin to experience pain, discomfort, or injury. This came to mind as I finished the chapter on identity. Working moms are more likely to adjust their identity to appease others or their profession rather than being unapologetically themselves.

One time I experienced this was when I was a consultant outsourced to a client site. The client had contracted my firm to provide onsite technical support for 20-30 hours per week. The first day I reported to the client site, it was obvious my presence was not welcomed. At our first meeting, one employee questioned why they hired a consultant to do work they could do themselves. Trying to ease the situation, I explained one benefit of using a consultant is that they could pick what they wanted to keep in house and give the tasks they didn't prefer to work on to me. He didn't buy it, resisted working with me, and refused to give me information needed to do my work there. I gave it a few days, but this person continued to make it a hostile work environment. I expressed my concern to my manager and was not given any options other than to figure it out. We didn't have another consultant available to assign to that site. I was disappointed that my concerns were invalidated, but the assignment was still an incredible opportunity for me to gain valuable experience. So, I endured the hostility and responded with kindness and humor to ease the tension. He eventually began to trust me and work more collaboratively with me. Our values didn't align too well so I didn't have an interest in becoming friends, but we developed a relationship that allowed us to work well together. It took about a month to get to that point. Their workload picked up, and they requested a second resource, so we subcontracted another local consultant. She also experienced friction with the same person who made my onboarding rough. He eventually warmed up to her too, but she did not appreciate some of his jokes and his comments made her feel uncomfortable. It made me realize that I had increased my tolerance in order to get by there. I shouldn't have had to, but that's what I felt like I had to do to if nothing was going to be done about the hostility and tension. It's the kind of behavior that led up to the #metoo movement that started a year later.

That same year, I was an exhibitor at a professional development conference. I made tiny potted succulent giveaways to get attendees to stop at our table. It worked and an attendee from a large, potential target client stopped by and grabbed one. The following day he texted me to let me know he dropped and potentially killed the succulent. I thought it was the perfect opportunity to setup an in-person discovery meeting and drop off a replacement succulent. I secured the meeting, and my firm was pretty excited at the prospect of landing this client. Things became weird when the prospective client started texting me in the days leading up to the meeting. At first the texts were work related, letting me know that he saw that we were already a vendor in their system. But eventually, the texts became more personal and he started flirting through texts. I let my manager know and he offered to take over. I politely declined because I thought I could handle it and I didn't want to give up a percentage of the sale because I needed it to hit my revenue target. I remember feeling as yucky about it then as I do now, but I believed I had the situation under control. I brought my manager with me to the meeting and it was awkward because the prospective client gave us a gift (something that they produced at the facility) and my manager kept awkwardly mentioning my husband to ensure the client knew I had one. The client awarded us a small project, and I became the project manager. Long story short, in an effort to secure a larger project/contract, I engaged in the flirting to the point that it interfered with my marriage. I was able to cut off communication before it got any worse. I gave it to my manager to take over because I was not willing to lose my marriage over a revenue target. I am not proud that I allowed it to continue to that point. But it is an example of how a job could cause you to change or lose your identity and become someone you're not if you are not aware, careful, or strong. It was a hard lesson to learn, but one I needed. I am much clearer because of it.

Feeling tangled is very closely tied to how aligned you are with your identity. As you align your V.I.B.E., check to ensure what is being asked of you in your various roles aligns with your identity. Things will move and flow when you are in alignment. Your energy, motivation, and eventually your V.I.B.E. will decline when you are not. Adjustments may have to be made to get in alignment, get moving, and get untangled.

Reflection

How aligned does what you are doing feel with your identity?

CHAPTER EIGHTEEN

When to Shift

ONE OF MY coaches taught me people only shift to gain pleasure or to avoid pain. If you want to convince someone to do something different, show how it will help them gain pleasure or avoid pain. In the last chapter I talked about being misaligned with your identity. I shared an experience of how dishonoring my identity (and my values) almost cost me my marriage and my family. It was a very uncomfortable and painful experience. Though I shared with you that I was not proud that I let it get to that point, I didn't explain how it got to that point.

That consulting job was the position that "rescued" me from my (not-so-pleasant) experience of working at the theme park. Transitioning from the theme park to the consulting firm felt like leaving an abusive relationship. The consulting firm offered me a position while I was experiencing the worst of what I experienced at the theme park. As much as I wanted to accept it right away, I was bound to the theme park for one year through the terms of my relocation package. If I left before one year, I would have to repay the money that the theme park paid to move our family. I explained this to my prospective new employer, and they offered to cover the cost to repay the relocation as a sign-on bonus. As much as I wanted to stay with the theme park and work things out, I knew it was affecting my mental health, and God was giving me a way out through this new opportunity. The consulting firm showed how much they wanted me to join the team by offering the sign-on bonus. It made me feel valued, something I definitely did not feel with the theme park. As painful and uncomfortable as that experience was, I embrace it as part of my journey.

I continued to feel valued when I started the new role. It was aligned with my values and it allowed me to honor my identity, at least in the beginning. It was very familial. The company encouraged work-life balance and was very intentional about personal and professional development and holding events to leverage and connect the different gifts and skills of the team. They valued, promoted, and lived diversity, equity, and inclusion. I was extremely grateful for the opportunity and the investments they made in me. I was motivated and set and exceeded goals to help the company grow. It was a mutually beneficial relationship.

Things changed when the company continued to grow and was acquired by a much larger, international company. The revenue targets of the new parent company changed the culture of the organization, and it became less focused on its people and more focused on revenue. Trying so hard to help this company that I felt indebted to be successful, I lost my identity. I felt the discomfort when it started, but I dismissed it. I continued to work through the discomfort until it turned into pain and the pain eventually turned into injury.

Recognizing discomfort and whether it is a symptom of growth vs. potential illness or injury is a valuable and necessary skill to have. Anything foreign or new can feel uncomfortable at first. With time and practice, it should get comfortable. If it doesn't, that should be your first indicator that the discomfort is a symptom of something more. When the discomfort doesn't dissipate and turns into heaviness or pain, that is your sign it's time to shift. That shift might need to be in your mindset, your perspective, or your environment. Questions to ask yourself are is your identity being valued and honored where it is? Does it allow you to be authentic? Do you feel safe? What shifts can you make to feel and be better aligned? Do not allow the inability of those around you to recognize your value to determine your worth. Do what you can to help them see it but if they just can't, make the shift before the pain turns into illness or injury. Take your skills and experience where they will be valued.

Reflection

Are there any shifts that need to happen to better align with your identity or for your value to be recognized?

"Don't be afraid to say no if it will cost you *energy* you cannot afford to give up."

WORKING MOMS
——— T R I B E ———

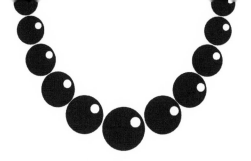

CHAPTER NINETEEN

Your Statement Pieces

I REALLY ADMIRE the late, former Associate Justice of the Supreme Court, Ruth Bader Ginsburg and how she so proudly stood for gender equity and against gender discrimination. I could not help but think of her and how purposeful she was when she selected her collars and jabots. She assigned a distinct message or meaning to each one and I imagine they each carried a distinct energy with them as she wore them. As I think of you, the working mom, reading this book, I am excited for you, who you will become, and what you will do when you get untangled. I send positive energy through this book to encourage you to find and refine your purpose and everything you will need for the journey. Every day, I will pray for every reader of this book. I pray that you will get your "necklaces" untangled, every skill, every experience, every identity you have been gifted along the way. As you align your V.I.B.E.

sorting them all out, may you recognize the meaning and significance of each one and embrace it. May you hold in high esteem the ones that were instrumental in getting you this point, polish them, and place them where you can easily reach for them again when you need them. May you wear them proudly and confidently when you need to channel the energy each carries.

Remember all the different "necklaces" you wore as a girl, a teen, a woman, a sister, a daughter, a friend, and mom. Hold and cherish the unique "necklaces" that were gifted to you when you became a mom. Never discredit how valuable every experience that made you a mom is. Others may try to minimize the mental, physical, and emotional journey you had to overcome to become a mom, even when they are benefiting from these valuable skills and virtues. You gave life to tiny humans, figuring out every skill needed to carry them to the next stage of their life, while adapting to how it changed yours.

Take time to go through the damaged "necklaces" and decide which ones you can repair and keep, and which ones no longer needed to be a part of your life. Find the purpose and value in the experiences that left you feeling tired, defeated, and broken. They are defining moments. You overcame and learned and eventually made it here. There is value in knowing that alone. You're still here because you have a purpose. God is not done with you yet.

Continue on your journey until that purpose is served, displaying and wearing your "necklaces" proudly. You will need them as you align your V.I.B.E., to prevent you from getting tangled, and to keep you moving forward. Create a system that reminds you where you've been and where you are going. It might be through morning affirmations, handwritten sticky notes, a whiteboard, your mirror, a vision board, listening to uplifting music, journaling, or a combination of these practices. Just be sure your "necklaces" are visible and easily accessible so when someone tries to tell you can't or you're not enough, you can confidently pull out the right "necklaces" and show them you can, and you are enough.

I used to be ashamed to wear some of my physical necklaces thinking they were too loud and drew too much attention. But as I aligned my V.I.B.E., I found my voice and know I need to use it to lift working moms who might not have found theirs yet. Now I wear my necklaces with conviction and purpose. I am excited for you to do the same and to experience the joy and freedom of being untangled.

Reflection

What "necklaces" do you want to wear proudly? What message(s) will you communicate as you wear them?

"I do not believe in coincidences because of how many times I have experienced the perfect answer to my *prayer* come at just the right moment."

CHAPTER TWENTY

Bless and Release

AS I ALLUDED in the last chapter, some "necklaces" you were only meant to have temporarily. They were only meant to teach you something or to carry you to the next phase or season. Be willing to let go when your "necklace" is done serving you and pass it on to someone else that might need it or just discard it. If the "necklace" no longer has meaning or significance to you or it has lost its energy, move on. It happens. Every relationship, job, opportunity, and challenge presented to you had its purpose for you. Some you will carry forever, others you only need until you don't. Recognize which are which. For the ones that you no longer need, acknowledge and give thanks for what they did for you, and release them. Holding on to things and people that no longer serve you blocks the things and people that are meant to be in your life from entering. You have finite capacity. Allow what is meant to pass pass and be patient, open, and ready for what is to come.

I mentioned in chapter 15 that I inherited the behavior of holding on to things for longer than I should from my parents. The same was true for relationships in my life. I have since recognized the shift in mindset that was needed to release them, but I am still a work in progress. As painful as they were, I released friendships that caused me more pain than joy. Every wedding anniversary, I reflect on the past year and who helped me and my husband grow, as a couple, that year. Sometimes I think back to our wedding day and think about our friends and family who were there but are no longer a part our life today. As I recall specific people, I think about how, at least at one point, they were a source of joy. I give thanks for those moments or phases and realize those are the ones I had to release so I can experience the joy with those I have in my life at the present. I get to decide what I keep from each of those experiences and I choose to only carry the happy memories and the lessons learned that will uplift me and energize me in the days to come.

I have become skilled at recognizing small people that don't deserve a permanent place in my heart or life. I am getting better at separating the small things from the giant experiences in my life that I still have much to learn from. Every now and then I still catch myself giving small things that don't matter more energy than they deserve. I still need reminders and for things to be put in perspective to remember what's small and what's not, what matters and what doesn't. Aligning my V.I.B.E. on a regular basis and daily morning prayer definitely help in that regard.

It can be challenging to release the things that no longer serve us, especially when we're comfortable. But if you know you've been somewhere for too long or put something off for longer than you should have, don't wait for things to get uncomfortable or painful. The release is the small step you can take to free yourself to get moving again.

Reflection

What are you holding onto that might be holding you back from amazing possibilities and the person you were meant to be?

"Those who genuinely *believe* they CAN will DO whatever they need to, even when they encounter a setback or adversity."

CHAPTER TWENTY-ONE

"Self" Talk

THIS IS A chapter dedicated to "self" because working moms notoriously forget to prioritize and focus on themselves. One approach I recommend trying to help you give yourself the same quality of care you give others is one I use to proactively manage employee health and safety. It involves listing the hazards a worker might be exposed to during the course of their workday and the measures (or controls) to eliminate or minimize exposure to the hazard. A hazard is anything that can harm you or put you in danger. When it comes to yourself, as a working mom, what are some of the hazards you are at risk of being exposed to? The ones that come to mind are self-doubt, self-sabotage, self-pity, and self-limiting beliefs. Many working moms give these hazardous behaviors way more power and energy than all the measures they can take to overcome them. Self-love, self-care, self-respect, self-awareness, self-esteem, self-confidence, self-worth. There are so many things we can do in these areas as preventive control measures, or self-empowerment.

Invest in yourself! Not only are you worth it, but the return on investment increases your value exponentially. You will see improvement in all levels and areas of your life when you invest in yourself. One small step you can take is to read more personal growth books just like this one. Find those that are specific for areas that have been a challenge for you or that pique your interest. Another way to invest in yourself is to find a coach or mentor that resonates with you and that has been where you are and where you are trying to go. They can hold you accountable and help to push you to or past your limits and outside of your comfort zone, where breakthroughs are made! Take classes to learn new skills. Be a lifelong learner. Investing in yourself will give you the clarity to be the best version of yourself. When you're the best version of yourself, you give the best quality care, output, and results to those around you. One of my favorite authors and speakers, Matthew Kelly, writes and speaks a lot about this idea.

I enjoy learning and it gives me the confidence to do my job better. Each time I pursued a new career, I researched what credentials and certifications would help me be successful in that field. I have three professional certifications that required so many hours of field experience, online and in person/classes, months of studying, and rigorous written exams. They also have annual dues and continuing education and recertification requirements. They are not easy to obtain or maintain, but they have helped my professional development in many ways. They demonstrate a certain level of proficiency and expertise to potential employers, stakeholders, customers, or clients. They have helped me stand out in the recruiting and hiring process and to increase my salary and negotiation power. I always negotiate personal and/or professional development into my total rewards package and offer letter. Employees who feel valued and appreciated are more likely to reciprocate and work harder. This is generally true for working moms and especially true for me. I am not hesitant to back my request with metrics and glowing performance reviews to show what they can expect to receive for the investment.

Prioritizing yourself is not selfish. It is responsible and resourceful. The quality of what you give and put out is only as good as the quality you put in. What you contribute will be best when you are rested, confident, energized, and feel appreciated. Taking the time to identify areas of opportunity for improvement and the steps you can take to strengthen those areas will not only benefit you, but everyone around you. Learning how to respect and value yourself will help you teach others how to respect and value you and set healthy boundaries so you can feel good about how you show up and what you produce. As moms, we are inherently selfless. It takes intention and practice to learn how to pour the same love and energy into ourselves as we do into others. It is a skill we can all benefit from mastering.

Reflection

How will you invest in yourself this week?

"Recognizing discomfort and whether it is a symptom of *growth* vs. potential illness or injury is a valuable and necessary skill to have."

WORKING MOMS
TRIBE

CHAPTER TWENTY-TWO

Fear Less

FEAR IS AN inherent response to the perception of danger. In nature, it helps protects animals from predators or potentially harmful situations. It's important to note that it is a response to the *perception* of danger, not to danger itself. My kids are afraid of the dark. If they are lying in bed, the room is not any more dangerous than when the light is on, yet they are still terrified. Fearing what you can't see is something that starts at a young age. If you don't learn how to face and overcome your fears, they will limit you from living.

Fear is one reason I encourage working moms to start the process of getting untangled and aligning their V.I.B.E. with dreaming big. Women who are tangled have forgotten how to dream with the pure, uninhibited heart of a child. Children are unaware of the barriers that might prevent them from achieving their dream, so they have no problem dreaming without limits. When I work with working moms, I have to remind them dreaming is exciting. I have to teach them that there is no commitment or expectation to take action or achieve their dreams. It's ok and encouraged to sit with a dream indefinitely and allow it to be a source of excitement and joy. Either it will lose its energy or continue to excite you at the thought of it. If it continues to excite you, it has a place in your vision. That's how you'll know it's time to make an action plan with goals to make that dream your reality. That's also when fear will try to tell you you can't or you're not enough. That is when skill is required to help you face and overcome your fears so you can reach your goals and vision.

Mel Robbins, author of *The 5 Second Rule*, teaches people how to turn their fear into excitement. She explains that fear and excitement elicit the exact same physical response in your body. The only difference is how your brain processes your body's response and decides what to do next. She teaches a technique of using her 5 second rule (counting backwards from 5 to 1 to activate the right part of your brain), focusing on a positive anchor thought related to what you are fearful of, and telling your brain repeatedly you are excited about that anchor thought. The anchor thought helps to keep your brain grounded, blocking the fear, anxiety, and irrational thoughts from overpowering you. It helps you stay in control of your thoughts and what you do next, acting out of excitement rather than fear. This aligns with the idea of always looking for the opportunity as I discussed in chapter 5. I am a Mel Robbins fan and recommend reading *The 5 Second Rule* if you haven't already!

Another way to overcome fear is to breakdown what you are fearful of into small steps. Usually, the smaller steps aren't as scary as the bigger outcome. Courage is built and confidence increases as each step is taken and overcome. Transitioning to a new role is a great example of facing a fear by breaking it down into steps. Deciding to leave a job for a new one can be scary, especially if it's one you have had for a long time. It may become necessary for several reasons. To make it less scary, you can break it into these steps: preparing your resume, researching new jobs, applying for new jobs, interviewing for new jobs, negotiating terms of the new job, resigning and/or negotiating counteroffers, and transitioning. Keep reminding yourself something to be excited about is what is on the other side of the fear. Hold onto the excited feeling until you get there. One step at a time, one victory at a time. I have a motto that I will be excited until I have a reason not to be. It has served me well so I will continue using it until it doesn't. You might be inclined to be discouraged if the first opportunity doesn't pan out. That just means it wasn't the right one for you. Continue to be excited for the right one that will come in its time.

After reading the mindset and identity chapters, maybe you've already realized that you need to develop a courage mindset. Learning how to take risks can help to develop that mindset. I have become risk tolerant because I have been rewarded by many of the huge risks I have taken. But I didn't start by taking huge risks, I started with small ones and worked my way to bigger ones. Through one of the career paths I chose, I learned how to assess and rate risks to make it easier to know which ones were safe to take. Thinking through the outcomes and how to make them safer helps to remove some uncertainty that causes fear. It also helps you decide if you can afford to take the risk or not. If you can afford to take the risk, if you can live without whatever you might lose, take the risk. If you cannot afford to NOT take the risk, if doing nothing will prevent you from having something that is essential to the life you want to live, take the risk. Taking the risks you can afford help you avoid regret.

Fear is at the heart of a lot of the things that cause us to become tangled. Learning how to overcome, or at least work through fear, is necessary to becoming untangled. Or depending which technique you decide to try, excitement can be at the heart of getting untangled! Start small, stick with what works for you, and give yourself time (and grace) to get better at it.

Reflection

How do (or will) you face your fears? What is one small fear you can commit to facing this week?

CHAPTER TWENTY-THREE

Enjoy the View

WHEN I GRADUATED from junior high, the school let our families publish messages to us in the yearbook. One of my messages came from my older brother. He told me to remember to stop and enjoy the view as I'm climbing up the mountain. This always feels so good when I take the time to remember to do it. As working moms, it is so important that we celebrate our wins as success, recognize our progress, and use it to push us to keep moving forward. In listening to working moms to find out why they might feel tangled, I often get the sense they don't feel successful. They speak as if success is something far in the future, something they've never achieved, or something they aren't deserving of. Survival, and not success, is their primary objective. I get it, I have been in seasons of survival mode.

What I want these women to know is that success is relative. No one else gets to decide or tell you if or when you are successful. You decide that. Success is accomplishing something you set out to accomplish. You have done this many times. Maybe you haven't reached your highest level of success (yet) but every small step leading up to it is a win, a success. As long as you haven't given up, you're not failing. Even when you make mistakes along the way, you're not failing, you're learning. Learning is part of growth. "Success" might be getting through the day or the week. When it is, and when you accomplish it, celebrate it!

I remember the day I resigned from my position with the theme park. It distinctly felt like failure. It made me uncomfortable in my own skin. It felt yucky. But I sat with it, it passed, and it strengthened me. It was a defining moment for me. I learned so many things from that experience. From that moment of weakness, my faith was made strong. I may not have stopped to enjoy the view at that moment, but I did keep going. I can stop and enjoy the view now, and see the places where I stumbled along the way, recognizing I had to pass through them to get to where I am. I couldn't see the top of the mountain from there, but I can see it now. I still have a long way to go, but I can see it.

If the word "success" strikes discord with you like "balance" strikes for some, as a term that only describes perfect working moms who have it all together, find terminology that resonates better with you. Success is simply a series of milestones, a measure of growth. Call it whatever you need to, but do not deny your success. Just because you don't feel successful, doesn't mean you're not. As long as you are measuring your progress using your own standard, not someone else's, and seeing growth, you are achieving success. Be proud. It's easy to confuse someone else's standard for yours, especially if you work closely, but you can't compare your progress to theirs. You aren't working with the same gifts or on the same vision. You're not in the same seasons of life and you haven't experienced the same opportunities and threats along your journeys. When you're so focused on other people's gifts, vision, or success standard, you are discrediting the work you've put in and walking the tightrope of self-doubt. It's a waste of energy that would be better spent focusing on your own journey.

Recognize and celebrate the wins, as small or grand as they may be. Even if they only last for a moment. They are the breadcrumbs sprinkled along the path of your journey. They are meant to encourage you to keep at it and let you know you're going the right way.

Reflection

What are three wins you can celebrate this year? It shouldn't matter how late or early in the year we are.

"I found my *voice* and know I need to use it to lift working moms who might not have found theirs yet."

WORKING MOMS
TRIBE

CHAPTER TWENTY-FOUR

Yes, You're Doing It Right

A BLESSING AND a curse of being a working mom is that every day you are put in situations that require you to figure out how to do something new, and you always do. The downside is as soon as you've mastered one thing, that season comes to an abrupt end and the next challenge is waiting in the wings. Every phase of your children's childhood or your career brings new opportunities to second guess yourself and question, "is this normal, am I even doing this right?" One of the best ways to learn and get good at new skills is to just start doing them. There's no handbook that could cover everything you need to know to be a good working mom. You aren't given a choice other than to learn as you go. You learn so many things along the way. At times, there can be so much coming at you, and so fast! The answer to your question is probably, no, it's not normal, but yes, you're doing it right.

Along with the gift of being a mom, and all the ups and downs that come with it, God gave you an incredibly unique ability with more power and utility than any skill you might learn from a book or online forum. It's your mom intuition. It is a strong gut feeling that gives you answers to many questions about what you should do. It can help steer you away from hazardous or unhealthy relationships or situations. It can also tell you to pursue something that all other reason would tell you not to. In the first chapter of her book *Believe It,* Jamie Kern Lima shares how trusting her gut led to an opportunity that changed the fate of her business and her life. Please read her book if you haven't already, her values and mission are so aligned with ours! So, between gathering information and following your mom intuition, yes, you're doing it right. As with every other skill and talent, learning to trust it and your own ability comes with time and practice.

There's a difference between when something is completely new to you and you have no idea what you're doing versus when you've tried a few things and have found what works for you. There will always be people, some with good intentions, some who think they just know it all, who will try to tell you you're doing it wrong. Protect your energy by avoiding people who insist on giving unsolicited advice or nod your head, smile, and take the advice with a grain of salt. If you can't, try to remind yourself: they don't have the same kids, job, partner, knowledge, resources, and skills that you have. There's a good chance things have changed since they did what you're doing. You know what's best for you!

My third child had severe eczema when he was a baby and toddler. It was all over his body and often on his face. We followed the doctor's orders and took him to specialists, dermatologists, and allergists. We tried every eczema cream recommended to us and explored different dietary restrictions. We were desperate, so there wasn't much we wouldn't have tried. It was mentally and physically exhausting and expensive to evaluate so many regiments. I finally found a homemade, essential oil recipe that his eczema responded well to and felt like we had it under control. Before that, I was an essential oil skeptic. Every essential oiler has their magic moment when they were sold on the power of essential oils. This was mine. But even though his skin was clearer, and he stopped experiencing flare ups, friends, family, and strangers would continue to give their unsolicited advice and opinions on how I was doing it wrong.

This happened when I resigned from the theme park as well. Everyone had an opinion on how I made a mistake by moving my family, put my family at risk by living so far from their school/our jobs, and how much I would regret giving up the perks and benefits of the job. By the way, I forgot to mention how many friends and family came out of the woodwork when I worked for this theme park. It was hard to tell which of those opinions were genuine versus the ones born of wanting free tickets to the park.

When my dear friend Martha was pregnant with her first and only son, her doctor saw an abnormality and advised her to terminate the pregnancy. Her intuition told her he was wrong, so she sought out two more opinions. They also told her both she and the baby would be at risk if she kept the baby, but her mom intuition was telling her so loudly that they were wrong. She decided to keep the pregnancy and delivered a healthy baby boy who is now ten years old. I have even heard of moms getting gut feelings to call or go to their children and check up on them when they were in danger. Mom intuition is a real and powerful thing.

You know what's best for you and your family. People may have pure intentions, but they are not wearing and walking in your shoes and living your life. They do not have to answer to the consequences of your decisions. What they are able to see is very limited to what you allow them to see. Their experience could not possibly be the same as your experience, even if similar. If your mom intuition is telling you to be strong and tough it out, it knows your breakthrough is right around the corner. If your mom intuition is telling you to get the heck out of there as fast as you can, it's trying to protect you. Gather information but trust your gut. It speaks to you to protect you.

Reflection

When was the last time your mom intuition guided you in the right direction?

"I will be *excited* until I have a reason not to be."

WORKING MOMS
——— T R I B E ———

"Holding on to things and people that no longer serve you blocks the things and people that are *mean to be* in your life from entering."

WORKING MOMS
——— TRIBE ———

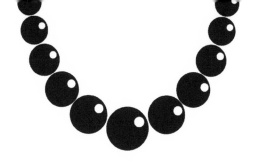

CHAPTER TWENTY-FIVE

Keep Showing Up

THE LAST TEN chapters have been very focused on you and your mindset and more ways to get untangled and discover or align your V.I.B.E. These last few chapters will be focused on how you show up and make your impact and the relationships in your life. They will prime you for when you're untangled and out in the world living your purpose and have identified the right habits that help you experience the clearest, highest level of your V.I.B.E.

We live in a world and an era that still tries to break us down, make us small, and tell us we, as women and moms, are not enough. Many people still believe our place is in the home, taking care of the home and children. This is despite the contributions we have made and continue to make in the workplace, in government, and in our world. As Ruth Bader Ginsburg put it, "Women belong in all places where decisions are being made." When I first started the Working Moms Tribe Movement, one of the primary objectives was to help career driven working moms move into leadership and executive level positions. As working moms joined the Movement and introduced themselves in our Facebook group, I learned that many of them were already at that level. A majority of them were very highly educated, experienced, and accomplished women. I thought it would have attracted moms earlier in their careers, possibly still in school, that were looking for an online community offering personal and professional development support specific to working moms. I was pleasantly surprised that the community quickly grew and with the breadth and diversity of perspective, experience, knowledge, and support the members were able to provide to each other. The community continued to grow rapidly because there was quality and value in the support the members gave and received.

There were a couple of things I found interesting about the dynamics of the community. First, it made me think that, generally, these working moms did not need the personal and professional development I wanted to offer them. Many of them were very driven and accomplished and knew what they needed to continue to move up. However, it was apparent they were tired and feeling burnt out in the process. Many of them were recognizing that, while the sacrifices and extra hours they were putting in gave them prestigious titles and more money, ultimately, they ended up with more work and even less time with their families.

I also observed that, like me, many of them had made it into leadership and executive level positions. Though they did seem proud of the accomplishments, they weren't enthusiastic about sharing their journeys of getting to those levels. Many were looking to step back or at options that were rewarding but less demanding.

This is what made me shift the focus of the Movement to working with employers to better understand the needs and situations of this class of workers (women who are moms) that constitutes a significant percentage of the U.S. labor workforce. There are tremendous benefits for both employers and their working families, and therefore their bottom line, if we can craft solutions that accommodate both the working moms' and employers' needs. Many organizations have recognized that Total Rewards systems that account for employee compensation, well-being, benefits, recognition, and development help to achieve business goals and increase organizational performance. The irony is that most organizations shy away from working mom specific accommodations or considerations because they might be viewed as discriminatory. Yet, through outdated norms and perceptions, working moms continue to silently experience and endure bias and discrimination that causes us to have to work harder as described above.

There is no denying that our collective efforts have moved us forward, but the data clearly shows we have a long way to go. What if we continue to run our race relay style? We might not have to show up, all in, all at once, but we should commit to continuing to show up. Those that feel tired and burnt out can pause or slow down to catch their breath. Those of that are untangled and armed with grace, strength, and clarity can continue to carry the baton to give the weak and tired some rest and recovery time until they are ready to rejoin the race that we are in together.

When life gets busy and stressful and wears you down, you might lose sight of your purpose and drive. It can make you feel like you're running the race alone. You might not see how the examples you are setting, or the opportunities created by what you are working on benefit your family or the working mom collective. It opens up another opportunity for self-doubt to creep in and affect your self-confidence and motivation. This is when, more than ever, you must grasp for those small easy steps to pull you through and keep you going. This is when knowing where to draw inspiration really matters. This is what it looks like to keep showing up. For you, for them, for us…it matters. So, take a deep breath, channel your V.I.B.E., see yourself on the other side, and find your way there.

As a former inspector of underground fuel storage tanks and again later as a health and safety consultant, my presence on site was not always welcomed. Depending on who I was working with, I could have been perceived as someone looking to cite and fine them, someone that was going to point out reasons they needed to spend money, or an overpaid additional resource. Sometimes when I was starting a new role, even coworkers weren't as welcoming as I had hoped. There were a lot of walls that were put up before the companies I inspected and regulated, clients, or coworkers got to know me and how I could be of benefit to them. They would ask me questions or challenge me to make me prove I knew what I was talking about. The objectives I was assigned to accomplish on paper were usually straightforward and doable, things I could figure out. It was the different layers of people I had to work with to accomplish those things that made my jobs challenging. I welcome challenge and sincerely believe you learn and grow through it, but some days it was exhausting, and I did not look forward to it. Some days I dreaded getting out of bed, thinking of all the personalities I would have to encounter in the day ahead. I hated the fact that so much of what I did was more about swaying buy-in than a collaborative effort to reach an objective.

When you get too caught up and tired with the day-to-day tasks it can get challenging to remember and see the bigger picture. If you can just remember that there is a bigger picture, that these small, seemingly mundane tasks and frustrating interactions have their place in it, and that whatever you have to give today is enough, you will reach a point that allows you to see the bigger picture again. Break it down before it breaks you down. I managed those days one project at a time, one person at a time, one conversation or email at a time. I may have felt like I was hitting a wall, but slow progress was being made. Things got done, unimportant things fell off, and objectives were met. It was not always neat, easy, or pretty. It was often messy. Looking back, there was learning, growth, progress, and even celebration. When you're tired, when you feel defeated, when you think it doesn't matter, remind yourself there is a bigger picture.

It's purpose, your purpose. If all you have the energy for today is only enough to complete tiny things, it is enough. Lean on your (our) tribe if you have to. Find inspiration, recover, regain balance, and re-energize. Do what you need to do, just keep showing up.

Reflection

What have you found to be effective at motivating or inspiring you to keep going when you feel like giving up?

CHAPTER TWENTY-SIX

Your Family Needs You More

YOUR FAMILY WILL always be your priority. This may not be palatable to your employer or colleagues, but it won't change the fact. This does not mean you will always want or need to put your family's needs before your career. This is just a reminder that you only have one family, and it is not replaceable. Jobs and careers are. The right one(s) for you will be the one(s) that allows you to live your purpose while being the mom you want to be. For one person it might be the one that pays the most, that has the most opportunity for growth, that offers the most flexibility, and the one that respects boundaries. For another person it might be the one that provides healthy challenges, gives respite from chaos at home, and fosters deep, meaningful conversations with other adults. Only you know what's best for you and your family. It might be a part-time job, or it might be a career that requires you to spend most of your time at work. What's important is that you know what this looks like so you can make it happen, and that you don't settle for anything less than you deserve.

Some employers are already supportive of working families so it may not take much to strike the right balance. Others may feel they should not have to adjust to accommodate your decision to work. In my early working mom years, I remember feeling uncomfortable and uneasy when I'd have to put in requests that had anything to do with accommodating my family. I worried that my employers would think I did not take my job seriously. I lacked skill and experience in those years, so my self-worth was low. With time, I gained skills and experience both as a mom and as a professional. I eventually found a balance that allowed me to feel like I was performing my role as a professional and a mom well, or I should say well enough. After several years, I eventually reached a point where I felt confident with my skills, experience, and the value I brought to my company. Feeling grateful and indebted to the organizations that hired me, I would take the time to genuinely learn my role and the organization and how I could be of the most value to them. Then I would work really hard to deliver value and exceed expectations. Not realizing I was doing it at the time, I would overcompensate so when I needed to take time off for my family, I felt like I had earned it.

Though this approach allowed me to take the time for my family when I needed it, I can't say I encourage it. I am achiever, and enjoy learning, and love a good challenge. So, this approach went will with that combination. However, many employers will take as much as you are willing to give and keep raising the bar until you push back. That can be dangerous for you if you are a "yes" person like I was. I learned a tough lesson on setting healthy boundaries because I had not developed the self-awareness yet. Yes, you should always bring value, but you should also have your priorities straight, and be willing to protect them! There is always a happy medium, for all involved parties.

Looking back, I used to question if the sacrifices I made, were the right ones to make. When I see the photos of the early years of my kids' lives that I missed because of my career, it makes me sad. Even though they don't remember, I feel like I should have been there on my older daughter's first day of preschool or many of my sons' field trips. It stung when I would make an effort to pick up my kids from school and their teachers didn't know who I was there to pick up because they hadn't seen me enough. I have to remind myself how all my collective experiences, good and bad, led me to getting untangled and finding my purpose. My direction could still change but it no longer feels like I'm running the same, meaningless loop. I still have to make sacrifices and balance family time with my professional life, but with much less resistance.

Your family needs you to be present mind, heart, body, and blessings. They benefit by learning from your example too. They are watching and learning how to interact with the world through you. They will learn a lot from school and may need you to reinforce what they learn there, but there are much more important life lessons they will learn from watching how you do life. They will learn how to respond to adversity from you. They will learn how to carry themselves and treat others. They will learn how to value themselves. Getting untangled is not only for you, but also for them. For them to get the best version of you and for them to learn to be the best version of themselves. So, if not for you, do it for them.

Reflection

Do you remember a time you observed your child do or say something that was a reflection of you? With this awareness, what lessons do you want to be more intentional about teaching them?

CHAPTER TWENTY-SEVEN

Community and Collaboration Over Competition

I'VE SAVED MY favorite and most important chapters for last, hoping they stick with you if there is anything you take away from this book. You are not alone and should not attempt to go on this journey alone. There are other moms experiencing similar opportunities and threats as you are. There are moms who have passed through the season you are in. You can share ideas on how to manage them better. Even if what worked for them doesn't resonate with you, there is comfort knowing it will pass. It's always easier, or at least more fun, to experience seasons with other women experiencing the same season. I've been pregnant alone and with dear friends. It was way more fun to experience the physical changes and mental and emotional challenges with someone else going through a similar experience.

There is someone else out there working 50–60-hour weeks (by choice), that can relate to and understand your want or need to do so. Or maybe you need someone who's lived that life to tell you it's not worth it. Find your person/people! They're out there.

It breaks my heart when this topic comes up in our Facebook Group. "I don't have time to find friends" or "my close friends and I have grown apart and are in such different places. I don't have friends that understand what it's like to be a working mom." It's hard enough being a working mom. To not have anyone to support, encourage, and lift you, or even worse, to have to waste energy explaining your decisions, would be not only lonely, but exhausting! No working mom should ever have to experience either scenario. Yet, we do. I invite you to join our online community to find your tribe. This community encourages the discovery and aligning of your V.I.B.E. as a working mom. We offer positive, uplifting support, encouragement, and authentic connection. If we aren't the community for you, the right one is out there, somewhere. What you put out, you attract. If you haven't found the right community yet, make sure what you are putting out there is consistent with what you are looking for.

The tribe for you will be the one that allows you to be unapologetically you, without having to second guess yourself. They will understand the season of life you are in because they are right there with you or they have been there before. They are strong for you when you are weak and will carry you on heavy days. They understand your choices and even if they don't or don't agree with them, they respect them. It's not about whether the "stay-at-home", "work from home", or "work outside of the home" mom way is better. Each choice comes with challenges and opportunities. The right choice is whichever option allows you to live your purpose while being the best mom for your family. Your way is not better than mine. My choice isn't superior to yours. We should all be better about finding how we can complement and support each other. Have an abundance mindset and know there is more than enough space and support for us all. We don't all have to like each other, but we should still hope for the best and lift each other. If we can't support each other, how can we ask others to support us and our cause? Together, we rise.

Reflection

Do you believe you have a scarcity or an abundance mindset? Is your natural tendency to compete or collaborate? Do you see a correlation?

"If you can afford to, *take the risk,* if you can live without whatever you might lose, *take the risk*."

CHAPTER TWENTY-EIGHT

Grace, Forgiveness, & Stewardship

FREE YOURSELF OF the pressure of perfection. If you're in a place, physically or in your own head, that makes you strive for perfection, try to shift to a place that fosters progress instead. What this might look like is using a vision as a starting point but not being tied to any particular outcome. Give, both yourself and others, the grace to grow in the process and trust that everything is falling into place exactly as it's meant to, despite how different it might look from your vision. There are often many routes and detours that can get you to the same destination. Be gentle with yourself when unforeseen roadblocks get in your way.

I love Brene Brown for the research she has done and her breakdowns of shame, guilt, and vulnerability. The emotions shame and guilt trigger can be painful and suffocating, leaving us feeling unworthy of the love and connection we need and deserve. Grace and forgiveness are what can carry you to the other side where love and connection can find and embrace you. Learning to give and receive grace and forgiveness are the best way loosen your ball of necklaces and keep it from getting so tightly tangled. They allow you to more easily let go of shame and guilt, which are unavoidable on our journeys. These areas may feel uncomfortable and yucky, but they help us build strength and character.

Stewardship and perspective can be another powerful combination. Previously I mentioned how changing your perspective, seeing things with a different lens, can help to better manage the opportunities and threats of your life when seeking recovery and balance. Responsibilities and obligations can feel heavy and weigh you down. A perspective shift that can help to lighten this load is to view everything in your life as temporary or borrowed. Instead of owning anything, consider yourself a steward of every gift, relationship, opportunity, and threat put in your life. Do your best to care for, manage and usher each as they pass through your life. Gently allow each one to fall into their place on your unique journey. As proud as I am of the various opportunities and roles God has entrusted me with throughout my career, I used to feel embarrassed by my list of work experience. I believed the lies that there were too many positions and that it was a poor reflection of me and my value. I had to learn to give myself grace and embrace my unique journey. Through it I was able to learn and grow and use what I learned to bless others. As imperfect and painful as it may have felt at times, I got to a place that allowed me to put this book in front of you today. I'm not finished, and neither are you.

Reflection

Are grace and forgiveness virtues that you can easily give and receive? Do you consider yourself a good steward of things entrusted to your care?

"If you cannot afford to NOT *take the risk*, if doing nothing will prevent you from having something that is essential to the life you want to live, *take the risk*."

CHAPTER TWENTY-NINE

Don't Take It Personal

ANOTHER REMINDER YOU might hear me give often to avoid getting tangled and to align your V.I.B.E. is to not take anything personal. Have you ever sent a text message and assumed the recipient saw your message when they didn't respond right away or at all? I know I've definitely come up with a list of assumptions that might explain why they didn't respond. They were ignoring me. They were mad at me. Then I try to go through all our recent interactions to find out which one it could have been. I assumed their lack of response had something to do with me. Why do we do that? Most of the time, your experience has nothing to do with you. Maybe their kid had their phone and opened the email or message. Maybe they were in the middle of something else when they received it. Maybe they are overwhelmed with other things going on in their life and it was outside of their capacity to respond at that moment. Maybe they had every intention of responding but just forgot. It happens notoriously on social media. Someone stumbles upon a cryptic post by a friend that is annoyed or frustrated by something or someone. Instead of addressing it, they vent about it on social media leaving several of their friends and family wondering if the post is about them.

When your first instinct is to take things personal, you can spend a lot of energy overanalyzing and figuring out how to respond. You might also take the conversation in a direction far from the original intent and objective. It's much easier to assume it has nothing to do with you. As nice as it would be if other people paid more attention to things you say, do, and share, you have to remember how consumed people are with what's happening in their own lives. Unless they make a conscious effort, it usually doesn't give them much time or energy to follow what's happening in your life that closely. Even if it is personal and intended to be directed at you, the fact that they couldn't come directly to you to discuss the issue says a lot about them and where they are in their journey. They may be too tangled or insecure to find the right ways to communicate with you. More often than not, an insecurity is the root cause. It's usually not that clear cut, but if that does turn out to be the case, then you can decide if and how much time and energy the situation deserves. Is it a potential opportunity to give grace or extend forgiveness? Or is there an opportunity to help each other learn, grow, and move forward. You might not be able to find the opportunity right away. Your path forward might be to bless, release, and find recovery in the areas of your balance that might have been affected. Either way, you can conserve energy by not being so quick to take things personal.

One of my bridesmaids didn't invite me to her wedding and I was pretty offended. I will admit, she wasn't one of my closest friends, but she was close enough to be one of the people in the delivery room when I gave birth to my first child. In the weeks leading up to the wedding, I did my best to not take it personal. I remembered how selective I had to be when determining our guestlist for our wedding. I was hurt that she didn't value our friendship the same way I did, but I understood. It was fine and probably would have passed, except the day after the wedding, she announced on social media how she stood before God and 250 of her family and friends and got married that weekend. In that moment, it felt like a punch to the gut and I could not help but take it personal. I started thinking about what I must have done to not make the list. I even went so low as to comment on the post, "Talk about pouring salt on an open wound!" I don't remember the exact sequence of events after that, but I know I stopped talking to her and wrote her an email expressing how hurt I was. I call it a "kiss of death" email. It's how I used to release people that I no longer wanted in my life. She responded to my email, to give an explanation, but I judged it as a lame excuse and wrote her off as a friend. In my mind, her leaving me off her pretty large guestlist was her way of communicating where we stood. I still don't know what the true reason was. The one in the email seemed more of an easy scapegoat. It could've been a financially driven decision, maybe her husband didn't like me, or maybe I did something to upset her. Whatever the real reason was she did not trust me or care enough to share it with me. Me spinning my wheels about it trying to figure it out wasn't going to change anything. The wedding had passed, and it helped to establish that we were at best, surface level friends. At least now there was a mutual understanding.

Conserve your energy for things that matter! Don't wait for life to place you in a circumstance that clearly delineates what's important and what's not. It's not about you, and even when it is, focus on the opportunity for learning and growth instead of the emotion that can't change the situation. Human nature may not allow you to recognize it in that moment, but as your purpose and V.I.B.E. become clearer, so does what's important and what's not.

Reflection

What was at the root of the last conflict you can recall? What is the lesson learned?

CHAPTER THIRTY

Heal Over Hurt

DURING ONE OF our Sunday masses, the pastor of our parish, Fr. John Amsberry, said, "If it's not transformed, it's transmitted. Hurt people hurt. Healed people heal." As you live your purpose, following your call, it's important to know, are you healed or are you hurting? Those you encounter along your journey, are they healed or are they hurting? Will they help you or hold you back? In the same way, the internet can be a powerful tool to help you with just as much potential to hurt you. Many hurting people turn to the internet when trying to ease the pain. Whether they intend to, they sometimes spread hurt. The internet gives hurting people a place to hide and cowardly spread hurt. In one of my neighborhood Facebook groups, I once came across a post that seemed like an opportunity to help someone. In the post was a picture of a bat hanging on someone's porch. The person who posted the picture asked for help to get rid of it. There were a handful of responses. Most of them advised the poster to leave it be and not disturb it. I commented and told her to check the local health department, as they may have a vector control division that assists with pests. I probably left out "pests that transmit diseases to humans". A few minutes later, someone responded to my comment and told me that bats are pollinators, not pests, and that I should educate myself. I responded with a link that gave information about the rise of rabies cases because of bats and what to do if you encounter a bat. I also informed her I received formal training and had the credentials to give the recommendation I did. What started out as an attempt to help someone quickly turned into bitterness. It shouldn't have, but it did. I should've followed my own advice, not taken it personal and kept scrolling. I was pretty tangled up at the time and needed to feed my own ego. I turned off notifications for the thread, so I do not know if it continued. Hurting people attack even the helpers and the healers. I would have responded to her differently if I looked at it from this angle, but instead, I came down with her and perpetuated negativity. I've seen other seemingly harmless questions or comments quickly spiral out of control because of one or two hurting individuals. Hurting people are not confined to the internet, but their reach extends so much farther and faster there.

We have the power to stop the hurt from spreading. When my youngest daughter was young enough to sit on our lap during flights, we would not purchase airfare for her. Most airlines allowed her to have her own seat if the flight was not full, so we would cross our fingers and hope the flight was not full. The last time we attempted to take advantage of this option, I asked the person checking us in if the flight was full. She correctly assumed I was asking if there was an extra seat our daughter might be able to take. She responded, "It's a full flight, and even if there is an available seat, I'd charge you for it." I thanked her for checking. She noticed there was one person in our party that had not checked in yet. It was my mom who had not yet arrived at the airport. I told her my mom would check in separately once she arrived. She assumed one piece of luggage we were checking in belonged to my mom. I don't know why she assumed that, we checked in fewer bags than the number of passengers we were. She proceeded to tell me it was against the law to check in someone else's luggage. She then attempted to explain why it was against the law. I interrupted her to tell her the bags we were checking in all belonged to us. I told her my mom would check in her own luggage upon arrival. Then she asked if we would be special checking in our stroller. I explained we needed it until take off. She shrewdly told me I had to gate check it in, assuming I was not aware. I finally asked her, "Why are you talking to me like this?" Immediately her tone and demeanor changed. She apologized and said she didn't realize she was coming off a certain way. Sometimes people who are hurting don't know that they are transferring their pain or frustration to others. Maybe she was just tired or maybe she dealt with a difficult person right before me. She was unaware of the negative ripple effect she could have caused. I was excited about the vacation we were about to begin so I had patience and did not respond in a way that could have amplified and transferred the hurt to more people. I easily could have. One small choice has the power to change the trajectory of a day, yours and others'.

A stranger in a car in front of me at a Starbuck's drive-thru randomly paid for my order one day. I was so moved by this random act of kindness that I continued the chain and have started it myself many times since. I don't know that I would have had the courage or idea to start one had someone not done it for me. But I remember how blessed I felt that morning and hope that I help someone to feel that too. Every day, every moment, we have the choice and ability to transfer hurt or healing. Guard your heart from hurt and always seek and spread healing. Find the healers that want to help you. Find healing in faith, the quiet and stillness of your morning, the laughter of your children, or wherever you can find it. In a world full of hurt, choose healing, both for yourself and for others. It's much easier to see and do when you're untangled. When you're there, be sure to share the rhythm of your V.I.B.E. loud enough so others ask how you're doing it. Start your own healing ripple effect!

Reflection

Do your thoughts, words, and actions come from a place of healing or hurting? What can you do to spread healing around you?

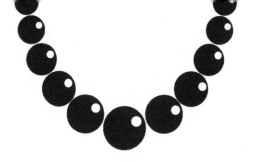

CHAPTER THIRTY-ONE

Be Kind. Be Happy.

YOU'RE NOT STUCK, you're not lost, you're not a hot mess. You may have been a little (or a lot) tangled because your purpose was unclear or you hadn't identified the right habits to help you overcome circumstances. But now you have the tools to untangle your "necklace" collection and leverage it to help you navigate through and around future circumstances. You simply start and start small. Find and align your V.I.B.E. to help keep you moving forward. Stay focused on your vision and leverage what inspires you to pursue it. Opportunities and threats may distract you, but by finding balance and energy you can stay (or get back) on track. It's a dynamic system that needs constant adjustment and reconciliation. Every day, a different element of your V.I.B.E. may require your attention. As you develop your habits, it will get easier to recognize where knots might be forming and what you can do to avoid getting tangled.

Getting untangled is very much a process of going through and purging your necklace collection, the skills, experiences, and identities you've picked up throughout your life. Be intentional about recognizing which ones to hold on to and which ones to let go of to make room for new ones that will better serve you. I shared what I have learned from my experiences and how they have helped me to align my V.I.B.E. as well as some of the habits that help me get untangled. I hope these experiences have given you ideas to help you discover and align your V.I.B.E. and the habits you will try or incorporate. They may not all resonate with you and for the ones that do, there may still be trial and error before progress. Intention and awareness will help you more easily recognize the ones that give you the best results. Those are the ones to focus on, practice, and refine. Define your own standard to measure your progress and remember to celebrate your wins along the way. There will never be a point or season in life where aligning your V.I.B.E. can't help you. Even when you've achieved "success", there will be a new phase of your vision to work on or the next best version of yourself to find. As long as you're still here, God's not done with you yet, you still have purpose.

At the very least, focusing on your purpose and aligning your V.I.B.E. will help release the things that are heavy and burdensome, lightening your load for your journey. If your steps still feel too heavy, they may not be small enough yet. They will get lighter as you become more skilled at aligning your V.I.B.E. or you may need to find ways to break the steps into even smaller ones. It takes time and practice to find the right groove and to feel confident with your new habits. Give yourself grace! The investment in yourself will be rewarding and help you to better serve your colleagues, friends and family. The confidence, courage, and clarity that come with being untangled will start small ripples that grow into big waves! I'm excited to hear about them.

I sincerely hope this book has helped you embrace every season of your journey, even the difficult and painful ones. Each gifted you with new "necklaces" carrying experience, skill, growth, or identity. There was and will continue to be meaning, purpose, and value. May you see your collection of "necklaces" in a new light, ready and proud to wear them as future seasons give you the opportunities to.

I want to end with the same message I send my kids off with daily. Be Kind. Be Happy. Don't steal anyone's joy and don't let anyone steal yours. When you're untangled, keep life light and simple by always choosing and promoting joy and not letting anything or anyone rob you of it.

Reflection

What do you feel inspired to do next?

For connection with other working moms aligning their V.I.B.E. or for additional support on your journey, join our online community or attend one of our live events.

www.workingmomstribe.org

Made in the USA
Middletown, DE
28 February 2022

61931960R00102